Deborah, Dee, Denise, denise forster, denise hunley, Deva Brockett, Diane, Diane D., Diane H., Diane Hope, dkidd2020, Donna Holmes, Donna Patterson, Donna S., donnaea, Doug, dukern74, Eileen Walsh, Elise, Eliza, Elizabeth, ELIZABETH AIRHART, Elizabeth Durand, Elizabeth Genco, Elizabetha, Ellen, ELLEN BERGGREN, Ellen Jones, ellen soppet, Elyse Meltz, Emidy Ritchie, Emily, Emily, Emily, Emily Kelton, Emily Parson, Emily Simnitt, Emily Tripp, EmilyHarris, Emma C., Emmy, Erika Varga, Erin Coscio, Erin McKinne, evonne, evonnewee, Florence Ward, Francesca, Francie, Francie Owens, Francie Owens, Francine Ferrara, Froukje de Ruiter, Gail, gail brown, gibsongrrl, Gillian Bidgood, Gina Russell, Grace, Grant Neufeld, grasshopper, Gretl Kramer, Gwen, gwynetho, gwynne lomen, Haley Parge, Hannah Condry, hazelpagoda, Heather, Heather, Heather, Heather James, Heather J., Heather Vering, Heidi, Heidi Butler, Heidi Ericson, Helen Hayes, Hila, Hillary, Hope, hpny knits, Illanna, isahaahs, Isela, Ive, ivywindow , J B, Jacey, Jackie Brown, Jaime, Jaime Robinson, Jaimie, Jan W, Jane, jane heldmann, Janet, Janet Gallagher, Janet Gattenby, Janet Killips, Janet Russell, JanetK, Janice Stenger, Janine, Janita James, Jason Meredith, Jazz Grady, jcasplund, Jen, Jen, Jen, Jen Kim, Jen Lushbough, Jenn_tx, Jenna Nicole Baker, Jennifer Bloxham, Jennifer Church, Jennifer Fay, Jennifer Halm, Jennifer Kogut, Jennifer Lindberg, Jennifer Manheim, Jennifer McBride, Jennifer MW, Jennifer Raab, Jennifer Sonnenberg, jennifmay, Jenny Boully, Jenny DeVasher, jennyoh, Jeremy Corona, Jess, Jessica, jessica Cheney, Jessica MacGregor, Jessica MF, Jessica Morris, Jessica Rose, jillz, jj heldmann, jmdp71, jo, jo strong, Joanna Ratcliffe, Jocelyn, Jocelyn_, Jodee DeBates, jodi, Jodi, Jody Scofield, John Collier, Joni Miles, joyce, Joyce, Joyce Greenfield, jrp1229, Jude, Jude, judy, Judy Boddy, Judy Ford, Julia, Julia Sprague, Julia Trice, Julie, julie every, Julie Kundhi, JulieFrick, jun, jupupedu, Kabira Kirby, kamsarmer, Kandy, Kara, kara paintner, Kara Walz, Karen, Karen Barbera, Karen Graffeo, Karen Heathcote, karen hesler, Karen Rapier, karrie Weaver, Kate Beesley,

knitalong

Celebrating the Tradition
of Knitting Together

LARISSA BROWN

MARTIN JOHN BROWN

To Sarah Gilbert

Published in 2008 by Stewart, Tabori & Chang
An imprint of Harry N. Abrams, Inc.

Library of Congress Cataloging-in-Publication Data
Brown, Larissa Golden, 1968-
  Knitalong : celebrating the tradition of knitting together / Larissa Brown and Martin John Brown ; photography by Michael Crouser.
     p. cm.
    ISBN 978-1-58479-665-7
  1. Knitting. 2. Knitters (Persons) 3. Online social networks. I. Brown, Martin John, 1966- II. Title.

  TT820.B83 2008
  746.43'2041--dc22

                        2007020908

Editor: Melanie Falick
Designer: Jess Morphew
Production Manager: Jacquie Poirier

The text of this book was composed in Century Schoolbook and Nimbus Sans.

Printed and bound in China
10 9 8 7 6 5 4 3 2 1

HNA ▮▮▮▮
harry n. abrams, inc.
a subsidiary of La Martinière Groupe

115 West 18th Street
New York, NY 10011
www.hnabooks.com

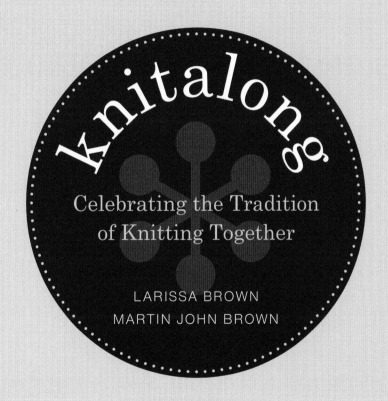

knitalong

Celebrating the Tradition of Knitting Together

LARISSA BROWN

MARTIN JOHN BROWN

PHOTOGRAPHY BY MICHAEL CROUSER

(unless otherwise noted)

STC CRAFT / A MELANIE FALICK BOOK

STEWART, TABORI & CHANG / NEW YORK

Contents

Projects

My First Knitalong

My first knitalong came early in my knitting career: It was the day I learned to knit.

Actually, I don't remember a specific day. What I do remember are long afternoons with my grandmother Olive. It was the 1970s, I was barely in grade school, and as I bobbed on the springs of her chenille couch, I worked obsessively on long rectangular strips. Sometimes I made garter-stitch slippers for Chet, my grandfather, who had "the sugar" (diabetes). My grandmother was in a zigzag phase, determined to leave a wide swath of New Jersey covered with acrylic chevroned afghans.

There wasn't any difference between knitting and knitting "together" when I was learning with Olive. It's the same for a lot of people today, no matter how old they are when they learn. That first day is a knitalong that can stay with a knitter for life.

"I'm kind of an oddball," comments Denise, a reader of the knitting blog January One. "It was my grand*father* who taught me to knit! The winter I was in fourth grade, Grandpa taught me how. I started with those little garter-stitch house slippers and then went on to knit for my Barbie dolls. I always think of his rough, worn hands gliding like silk when he knit."

Leslie, a knitter and homemaker from Pittsburgh, learned from her mom when a beach vacation turned rainy and all the guys split for home. "We sat in our jammies every day until the afternoon, watching movies and knitting," she says. "Honestly, that is all I can remember doing for that couple of weeks. Maybe stopping to sleep and eat—maybe," she jokes. It was a special time she'll never forget.

"I learned how to knit thanks to my ex-boyfriend," writes a blogger named Kadi, "who had been taught as a child by his mom. I remember him showing me, and the two of us just sitting in bed together, talking about our day and both knitting."

The same ingredients occur in these stories again and again. There's a knitter with a relative or a friend, together with that rarest of things: a long, drawn-out chunk of hours with little to do. A woman on a flight to Iceland finds the in-flight movie unwatchable and learns from her seatmate. Friends hole up in a riverside cabin; two knitters go in, three come out. An English sailor on the Indian Ocean in the sixteenth century sits down on deck, and a Tamil cabin boy shows him the needles. Knitting is an art that has been transmitted from person to person for centuries, and when knitters teach and learn, their friendships get richer, too.

Maybe taking up knitting is some sort of declaration that life should include more quiet hours and friends. A knitalong can help you find both.

The term *knitalong* emerged out of the Internet knitting culture of blogs and discussion groups around 2003 and 2004, when it was used most often to describe the practice of knitters in different places working on the same project during the same time period. While they didn't all turn on their computers and knit at the same moment, they did pledge to make the same scarf, socks, or sweater pretty much simultaneously.

In this book, my coauthor (and husband) Martin and I expand the meaning of the word knitalong a bit. We define a knitalong as any organized event where people knit together for a common purpose or goal. There are thousands of such events going on every day. To name a few that appear in this book, a *knitalong* can be:

- knitters meeting in a café, gossiping and working on whatever projects they want
- professional hand-knitters gathering by a fire, singing songs, and telling stories to decrease the drudgery of piecework
- hundreds of people knitting the same hat pattern and posting pictures of their work on the Internet in a friendly competition to show the wittiest and wildest embellishment
- knitters from around the United States working on entries for their own county and state fairs and reporting progress on their personal blogs
- fiber artists collaborating internationally, using satellite weather data, traffic patterns, and yarn
- knitters collaborating via the postal service to construct blankets and hats for survivors of war and disaster
- and a thousand other things

There are so many variations on the knitalong idea that Martin and I couldn't possibly cover them all.

Instead, we bring you fifteen essays that profile the variety and richness of the ways people knit together and the reasons knitters find it so worthwhile. Along the way, we tempt you with twenty projects inspired by those stories—projects especially suited to the knitalong treatment.

For six of those projects, we've run knitalongs of our own. My Knitalong Diaries give some inside details about the experience, while photo galleries of just a few of the finished objects represent the dozens, sometimes even hundreds, of volunteer knitters who participated. We love the way different knitters working from the same pattern produce finished objects that are so remarkably individual, so we've posted the entire galleries for you to visit at knitalong.net.

The book is organized according to the basic experience a knitalong provides for today's knitter. For example, Chapter 1 is about the simplest knitalong experience of all: hanging out with other knitters. After a brief introduction, we paint three specific scenes from the knitalong world: the burgeoning trend of knitting cafés, the time-honored tradition of knitting meet-ups in homes and nightspots, and the occasional knitting spectacle, like Stitch N' Pitch night at major league ballparks.

We match up these stories with patterns like the Doppio Gauntlets and Pinwheel Blanket—patterns that are elegantly simple, so you can focus on the cocktails, or the ball game, and still not have to rip out mistakes when the night is over. For the Pinwheel Blanket, we ran our own very casual knitalong, resulting in a gaggle of blankets as diverse and individual as the people who made them. We share photos of a few along with my pinwheel diary.

Chapters 2 through 5 work much the same way. Chapter 2 takes time for remembering some of the knitalongs of the past and the reasons for them. For some, knitting used to be more job than beloved pastime. We sketch creative ways that peasants tried to reduce the drudgery of knitting socks for a living, and pair those stories with a simple sock pattern and knitalong story of our own: Socks 101, a project that helped some of our fellow knitters get over the fear of turning their first heels. A story about orphans who were compelled to knit for their own self-improvement is matched with our Victorian Baby Bonnet pattern. The chapter ends with an essay about the best-known reason for knitalongs: war. We contrast wartime sock drives with a contemporary knitalong and pattern that is a prayer for peace, the Felted Peace Crane from the knitnotwar 10o0 project.

Projects like knitnotwar 10o0, which produce multiple copies of a single design, show just how unique the work of individual knitters can be, even within the constraints of a pattern. Chapter 3 revels in this phenomenon, celebrating ways knitalongs can help you find your own voice as a knitter. Our Meathead Hat pattern invites you to take a simple pattern and make it your own with color and embellishment, and the variety in our Meathead Hat gallery shows a sample of how far those simple choices can take your work. Alternatively, you could express yourself by writing about knitting on your own online "blog." The Pillow of Sei Shonagon is a project that invites you to celebrate beauty and the written word, taking inspiration from an ancient Japanese courtier who might just be the original blogger.

Chapter 4 delves into knitting together as a great milieu for growing in skill and confidence. Other knitters can buoy you when you feel swamped by a new technique, or they can egg you on to try something you're scared of. Challenge-oriented knitalongs like the Knitting Olympics would be a great time to test yourself with the two-color stranded knitting in the Entomology Hat and Mitten Set. When we encouraged knitters to stretch their abilities by putting their work into competition in our State Fair Knitalong, we inspired, among other things, a blue ribbon-winning Scrap Wrap, reprinted here. Finally, we tell a story of knitters growing together through collaboration, and we offer the Blessingway Blanket as a possible joint venture.

Giving has always been at the heart of the knitalong experience, and is the subject of Chapter 5. Sometimes every click of the needles is a little prayer that a knitted object can make someone's life—and maybe even the world—just a tiny bit better. There are a million kinds of generosity, but here we look at just three. Gifting among friends is eternal. A Knitter's Magic Yarn Ball is a perfect bonbon of love for that most special friend—a fellow yarn lover—while the Traveling Scarf is eye candy for anybody. Still, these days it's not just friends who need your gentle touch, it's the whole earth as well. We match a story about environmentally aware crafting with a pattern for a sweet Recycled Sweater Pincushion. Last but not least, we look at the world of knitting for those in need with a focus on the simple, powerful, knitted afghan square.

If all these stories have gotten you itching to start a movement of your own, Chapter 6 winds up the book with a practical DIY guide to launching your own knitalong, based on interviews with successful knitalong organizers and experiences Martin and I have had over the past several years.

Over that time, I've found that knitting together can be inspiring, supportive, hilarious, solemn, and even world-changing. Knitalongs, regardless of setting or scale, are about being together, being human, and about a reverence for what other people make. My grandmother Olive isn't with us now, but if she were, I'm sure she'd be surprised we even needed to write a book about knitalongs. For her, knitting together with family and friends was the obvious, and usually the best, way of doing it.

—Larissa Brown, Portland, Oregon

9

FAQs About KALs

People have been knitting together for centuries, but *knitalong* is a new term, and many knitters are still confused about what it means and how it relates to the Internet. While this book demonstrates that a knitalong can mean a whole range of things, here is a quick fix on some of the most frequently asked questions (or FAQs in computer lingo) about the subject.

Q: What exactly is a knitalong?

A: Any organized event where people knit together for a common purpose or goal. The term began its life on the Internet in the early 2000s, but we are expanding it to include non-Internet knitting, too.

Q: Are there more knitalong opportunities if I have Internet access?

A: Definitely. Some knitting circles post schedule changes and other information on the Internet, even though they meet in person. Some knitalongs, like the Knitting Olympics (see page 102), are entirely Internet-based. In general, the Internet is a huge part of today's knitalong culture.

Q: Am I required to have my own website or blog to participate?

A: Only rarely. The great majority of online knitalong events require only basic Internet access, not a blog for each participant. The organizers of each knitalong set their own guidelines and will usually state "the rules" up front.

Q: How do I find a knitalong I might want to join?

A: Finding a KAL online is as easy as using a search engine, such as Google.com, and typing in "knitalong" and perhaps the year or type of project you're interested in finding. To find an in-person KAL in your community, the best place to start is your local yarn shop or an on-line group that is focused on your town or city and may provide a meet-up calendar.

Q: Why are the Internet and knitalongs so connected?

A: The Internet in all its forms—websites, blogs, e-mail, podcasts, and a dozen more modes of communication—is more than a source of free knitting patterns. As you'll see, it enlarges your circle of knitting acquaintances beyond the borders of your town—way, way beyond to other countries and continents. It can help you find and communicate with your knitting peers: the people who are working on exactly the same sock or shawl, or who can help you finish that unfinishable neckline; the people who appreciate what you're doing more than your spouse does; the people whose knitting inspires you. It doesn't matter if they live in New Hampshire or New South Wales. Most of the galleries and knitalongs in this book would not have happened without that kind of communication.

Q: So what's up with all the jargon?

A: Knitters typing away at their computer keyboards are constantly coming up with abbreviations and slang. Here are a few of the terms that may come up as you read our book or surf the Internet for online KALs:

Blog—an online diary, or weblog

KAL—knitalong

LYS—local yarn shop

WIP—work in progress

FO—finished object

UFO—unfinished object

Frog—to rip out a knitted work ("rip it, rip it")

Tink—(knit spelled backward) to "unknit" a few stitches—less intense than frogging

Podcast—a sort of online radio show, most often independently produced by people who are passionate about a subject, such as knitting, and distributed freely

Swap—used online, this term describes any organized official penpal-type trade

Chapter One Hanging Out

There's something timeless about sitting around with your fellow knitters and your works in progress. The warmth of a fire or a cup of tea, the clicking of needles, and the satisfaction of quiet talk—or no talk at all—has a completeness to it. Nothing more need be added.

It's an experience you share with nearly every knitter from nearly every time and place. Digging around in old travelogues, you might unearth a quote like this:

"I was tempted, after breakfast, into the ladies' cabin," wrote the intrepid female traveler Matilda Houstoun from a ship in the Gulf of Mexico in 1845, "where I remained because I was pleased and amused by what was going on. The wife of the captain . . . took great pains to teach me the art of knitting, in which she was wonderfully skilled, and I in return, answered her questions about England."

Something about knitting seems to make it easier to listen and bond. When Matilda left the ship, the captain's wife gave Matilda the hat she had been working on. Matilda was charmed—she prized the hat "as a proof of kindness and good feeling." It was just one of a thousand friendships that have been sealed by knitting, much to the bafflement of less crafty types.

Today the experience is much the same—though it doesn't often happen by coal fires or in creaking ship cabins. This chapter looks at three places knitters are hanging out today.

Cafés dedicated to knitting and knitters are burgeoning in popularity. Combining a yarn shop with a casual venue to knit, eat, and chat means you have a dependable way to satisfy your craving for knitterly company.

Knitting circles and meet-ups can be found in every size and level of intensity, from intimate get-togethers of just a few friends, to a dozen or so gathered for a local stitch 'n bitch, to knitting "services" of the Church of Craft

with enough participants to fill a lecture hall. These meet-ups are a way to see the same set of knitters again and again, compare progress on projects, and make friends along the way.

Finally, there are times when knitters just want to make a spectacle of themselves. Events like major league base-

ball's Stitch N' Pitch and Worldwide Knit in Public Day take knitting to the front and center of people's attention. For some it's just a good time, but for others it's a way of coming out of the closet and saying, "I knit and I'm proud."

At knitalongs like these, you want projects that interest you but aren't so complex they make it hard to socialize. When you set out to knit among friends, it's good to have a lot of simple work to knit on. Consider projects like the Doppio Gauntlets, French Press Cozy, or Olive's Afghan. And last but not least, Genia Planck's mesmerizing Pinwheel Blanket is the basis for the first of Larissa's Knitalong Diaries, where you'll discover how a simple pattern can yield a flowering profusion of perfect little blankets, leaving knitters with a lot to be proud of, and just as good, a lot to talk about.

Knitting Cafés

Sarah Hickerson has lived in a lot of interesting places in her life, from the rolling hills of Tennessee, to the Isle of Man in the Irish Sea, to two years in a tiny West African village called Koundian, on a stint for the Peace Corps. But nowadays she's spending a lot of time on the couch in the back of Mabel's Café & Knittery in Portland, Oregon. Sarah is a labor and delivery nurse-in-training at a public hospital, and Mabel's is a "knitting café"—a combination yarn shop and coffee bar. For a knitter with an extraordinarily stressful job, Mabel's is a perfect refuge. Most of the time, just being there is all the knitalong Sarah needs.

"I'm not just a regular, I'm *the* regular at Mabel's," she jokes. Three or four mornings a week you'll find Sarah on that couch, surrounded by cubbyholes overflowing with wool, cotton, and silk goodness, enjoying a double soy latte—an order the staff has memorized.

Though Mabel's can get busy in the morning serving commuters with coffee (in the evening, classes and groups can order beer, cake, and wine) there's a palpable calm to the place. For some reason, wireless signals for phones don't work well inside. People tend to tuck their devices away to beep another time. It's a place just a little bit removed from the world, which means it's the perfect place to play with yarn and enjoy sympathetic company.

Sometimes Sarah works quietly on one of her impulsive knitted projects, like the giant felted beet she's making for a neighbor's toddler. Sometimes she chats with whoever comes by. Usually, she does both. Her company over at the café tables might be an eight-year-old devouring a cookie and up to his elbows in a glittering fuzzball of novelty yarn, a group of glamorous women sharing tea and plucking away at scarves, or a new mom reaching around the curve of her slinged newborn to work a purl row. And if any of these knitters runs out of supplies or discovers a problem—with their double espresso or with the cable they're working—the staff is right there to help.

Sarah might be a little more enthusiastic than most, but she's hardly alone in her love for knitting cafés.

In recent years, knitting cafés have been popping up like dandelions on a summer lawn. Of course, people have long hung out around the big, inviting tables at yarn shops, or gone to knitting classes and events featuring food and drink. And in the United Kingdom and Japan, weekly or monthly knitting parties are often sponsored by restaurants or coffee shops.

But the full-time yarn shop and café combination is a relatively new and North American phenomenon. Suzan Mischer's Knit Cafe in Los Angeles was a pioneer, opening in 2002. Unlike traditional yarn shops, which vary in the degree to which they encourage industrious loitering, Knit Cafe was designed for full-time hanging out. "I just wanted to have a place where I had the music I loved, a cup of coffee and a relaxed, laid-back atmosphere," Suzan told the *New York Times*.

The idea spread. In New York, The Point Knitting Cafe asks customers to "eat, knit, and be happy." In Maine, the Knitting Experience Café beckons with its big red couch. North of Seattle, Washington, Village Yarn & Tea Shop

specializes in tea alongside their cottons and cashmeres. Some, like Close-Knit Cafe in Louisville, Kentucky, offer free wi-fi for those who want to surf the Internet while they sip amid the fibers. At Lisbet's Knitting Cafe in Doylestown, Pennsylvania, the coffee and tea are complimentary. And at the Sow's Ear, a knitting store and coffee shop in otherwise quiet Verona, Wisconsin, late-night knitting eves have been expanded due to unexpected popularity.

No matter where these cafés bloom, the basic idea is the same. Knitting cafés aren't just places to buy yarn, they're places people can meet and knit in comfort and company, and maybe even cross a few paths with people they'd never meet if they didn't have knitting in common.

"Conversations start with 'What are you knitting?' but from there, anything can come out of your mouth," quipped James, a New York fitness instructor and knitting café patron, to *US News & World Report*. Jocelyn, a knitter and photographer in Calgary, has a habit of going to a knitting café once a week, partly to meet people she *doesn't* have a lot in common with. The bond of knitting is enough to start a conversation, and tea and cupcakes don't hurt, either.

Knitting cafés strike a rare balance between a completely public site—where whipping out your knitting needles might make you stand out like a wayward purl on a field of knit stitches—and staying at home, where you can be yourself but surprises and inspiration are harder to find. At a knitting café, there is no shortage of supplies or advice. If you run into a problem, you can duck over to the counter for advice or grab a row counter from the sale bin.

It's such a perfect combination that for Liz Tekus, the owner of the Cleveland, Ohio, yarn store Fine Points, adding a tearoom to her shop was a natural evolution. She saw how much her customers were getting out of their interactions at the store. They were lingering, talking, and hanging out in the backyard, even though it wasn't officially part of the store. Casual encounters were becoming real friendships.

"Some of these women have serious things they're going through," Liz says, listing a few: divorces, sons at war, illness. The camaraderie of knitting together was obviously a great pleasure and relief for them. Rather than crack down on their loitering, Liz made a space for them to revel in it. "This is a place where they can escape from their lives," she says.

Back on her couch, Sarah Hickerson would probably agree. The scene at Mabel's—long stretches of peaceful work and conversation, without pressure to produce and compete—reminds her of the pleasant gatherings of women in Koundian, her Peace Corps village.

"It's a coming together of people, where we can sit and time doesn't really matter," she reflects. She'll have to go back on the clock and help deliver some babies tonight, but in all likelihood, she'll be back at Mabel's tomorrow. She's got a crazy idea for a knitted boat she wants to bounce off some sympathetic fellow crafters, and at Mabel's, she's pretty much guaranteed to find them.

Sipping and Stitching Around North America

Here are a few of the many knitting cafés that can be found in North America:

....

Abundant Yarn & Dyeworks, 8524 SE 17th Ave., Portland, Oregon; 503-258-9276; www.abundantyarn.com

Fine Points, 12620 Larchmere Blvd., Cleveland, Ohio; 216-229-6644; www.finepoints.com

Fringe! A Knit Cafe, 823 E. Third St., Tulsa, Oklahoma; 918-382-0411; www.fringe-cafe.com

Knit Cafe, 8441 Melrose Ave., Los Angeles, California; 323-658-5648; www.knitcafe.com

Knit New York, 307 E. 14th St., New York, New York; 212-387-0707; www.knitnewyork.com

The Knitting Experience Café, 14 Middle St., Brunswick, Maine; 207-319-7634; www.theknittingexperience.com

Knit One Chat Too, #509, 1851 Sirocco Dr. SW, Calgary, Alberta; 403-685-5556; www.knitonechattoo.com

Lisbet's Knitting Cafe, 123 W. Court St., Doylestown, Pennsylvania; 215-230-9970; www.lisbetsknittingcafe.com

Mabel's Café & Knittery, 3041 SE Division St., Portland, Oregon; 503-231-4107; www.mabelscafe.com

The Point, 37a Bedford Street, New York, New York; 212-929-0800; www.thepointnyc.com

The Sow's Ear, 125 S. Main St., Verona, Wisconsin; 608-848-2755; www.knitandsip.com

Village Yarn & Tea Shop, 19500 Ballinger Way NE, Shoreline, Washington; 206-361-7256; www.villageyarnandtea.com

The Yarn Garden Sipperie, 1413 SE Hawthorne Blvd., Portland, Oregon; 503-239-7950; www.yarngarden.net

Doppio Gauntlets

Any knitting café worth its salt should be able to serve you a doppio con panna, *or double shot of espresso with whipped cream, and this pair of arm warmers is reminiscent of nothing so much as that sweet little drink. They deliver a double shot of two colors of luscious yarn swirled together using simple cables, and are topped with a frothy, creamy edge of a special bulky wool. Delicious.*

FINISHED MEASUREMENTS 7" circumference at wrist; 10" circumference at elbow; $14^1/_4$" long (to fit average adult woman)

YARN Malabrigo Worsted (100% merino wool; 215 yards/ $3^1/_2$ ounces): 1 hank each #181 Marron Oscuro (A) and #161 Rich Chocolate (B); Blue Moon Fiber Arts® Leticia (100% handspun wool; approximately 80 yards / $3^1/_2$ ounces): 1 hank Spring Fling (C)

NEEDLES One pair straight needles size US 9 (5.5 mm). Change needle size if necessary to obtain correct gauge.

NOTIONS Stitch marker; cable needle (cn)

GAUGE 16 sts and 24 rows = 4" (10 cm) in Stockinette stitch (St st) using A

NOTE
Colorways that are similar such as those shown, will blend subtly. The more different your colors are from one another, the more they will stripe.

Abbreviations
C6F: Slip next 3 sts to cn, hold to front of work, k3, k3 from cn.
C6B: Slip next 3 sts to cn, hold to back of work, k3, k3 from cn.

Stripe Pattern (any number of sts; 4-row repeat)
*Work 2 rows with A, then 2 rows with B.
Repeat from * for Stripe Pattern.

RIGHT GAUNTLET
With Long-Tail CO Method (see page 156) and C, CO 28 sts.

Cut yarn, leaving a 5" tail. Begin Stripe Pattern; work throughout entire Gauntlet.

BEGIN CABLE PATTERN
Rows 1 and 5 (RS): p11, K6, p11.
Rows 2, 4, and 6: K11, p6, k11.
Row 3: P1, yo, p2tog, p8, place marker (pm), C6F, p8, p2tog, yo, p1.
Repeat Rows 1-6 until piece measures 7" from the beginning, ending with Row 4 or 6.

SHAPE GAUNTLET
Increase Row (RS): P3, m1-p, p3, m1-p, purl to marker, k6, purl to last 6 sts, m1-p, p3, m1-p, p3–32 sts.
Work even until piece measures 8" from the beginning, ending with Row 4 or 6.
Repeat Increase Row–36 sts. Work even until piece measures 10" from the beginning, ending with Row 4 or 6.
Repeat Increase Row–40 sts. Work even until piece measures 14", or desired length to elbow, ending with Row 6. Cut yarns, leaving 5" tails.
Change to C. Knit 1 row. BO all sts loosely knitwise.

LEFT GAUNTLET
Work as for Right Gauntlet, working C6B instead of C6F on every Row 3 of pattern.

FINISHING
Laces: Cut two pieces of C 3 yards long. Beginning at wrist, thread one piece through eyelets of each Gauntlet as if to lace a shoe. Tie bow at elbow.

French Press Cozy

There's something romantic and pure about deep, dark coffee in a glass French press. It conjures up visions of canal-side cafés or brisk, breathtaking campsite mornings. But the reality is that coffee in glass gets cold awfully fast. Generations of knitters figured out a solution for the tea crowd, and now this twist on the classic tea cozy will keep your coffee toasty while you sip over a long and deep conversation. Clean rectangular panels and a knitted-on I-cord edging reflect the mod designs of most French press pots, while a winding I-cord closure recalls the steam rising off your favorite poison.

YARN Abundant Yarn & Dyeworks Kona Superwash (100% superwash wool; approximately 100 grams / 245 yards): 1 hank hand-dyed by Abundant Yarn's Jenna Smaniotto using Stumptown Coffee Roasters coffee grounds as dye

NEEDLES One pair straight needles size US 4 (3.5 mm); one set of three double-pointed needles (dpn) size US 3 (3.25 mm). Change needle size if necessary to obtain correct gauge.

GAUGE 26 sts and 37 rows = 4" (10 cm) over Ribbing Panel with larger needles, slightly stretched

NOTES Instructions are given for a 1-liter French press with a circumference of 12" and a height of $6^1/2$" from below the handle to just below the top lip. To modify the pattern for a different size Cozy, measure your press's circumference and height. Each ribbing panel measures 4" across when lightly stretched. Work the number of panels that creates a circumference that is about 1" smaller than your press's actual circumference. Add or remove columns of ribbing to achieve an exact desired measurement, but always begin and end each right-side row with one knit stitch.

Basic Ribbing Panel (multiple of 26 sts + 1; 1-row repeat)
Row 1 (RS): K1, *p2, k3, p3, k5, p3, k2, p2, k3, p2, k1; repeat from * to end.
Row 2: Knit the knit sts and purl the purl sts as they face you.
Repeat Row 2 for Basic Ribbing Panel.

COZY
Body
With larger needles, CO 79 sts. Begin Basic Ribbing Panel. Work even for 4 rows.
Eyelet Row (RS): K1, p2tog, yo, work to last 3 sts, yo, p2tog, k1. Work even until piece measures approximately 6" from the beginning or to $^1/_2$" below top lip of French press, working Eyelet Row every 8 rows, and ending with an Eyelet Row. Work an additional 5 rows of basic ribbing pattern. BO all but the last st.

I-Cord Edging
Slip last st to smaller dpn, using Backward Loop CO (see page 156), CO 2 sts–3 sts on needle. Work I-Cord (see page 156) for 1 row. Turn Cozy so WS is facing you. Work Applied I-Cord (see page 156) around BO edge, right edge, CO edge, and left edge, making sure to pick up sts evenly. When I-Cord ends meet each other, leave sts on needle for bind-off. With second dpn, pick up 3 sts from beginning of I-Cord; graft to end of I-Cord using Kitchener Stitch (see page 156).

I-Cord Tie
With smaller needles, CO 4 sts. Work 36" I-Cord.

FINISHING
Block lightly, being careful not to over-stretch ribbing. Weave in ends. Position Cozy on French press and lace up ties like a corset. *Note: If you machine wash the Cozy, do so in a lingerie bag to protect the I-Cord.*

Knitting Circles and Meet-Ups

Elizabeth was back in Portland, Oregon, after some long years out of the country. She wasn't shy about admitting it: She wanted to make some new friends and do something new. And she had always wanted to knit socks. Never mind that she had never knitted even a dishrag. All she needed, she figured, was a knitting group.

It wasn't hard to find one in this craft-obsessed city. She asked at local yarn shops and trolled Internet sites and found dozens to choose from. She tried a group that met at Starbucks every Sunday afternoon. Some of the members were experts, others less experienced, but they didn't really mind that Elizabeth was starting her knitting career with a fairly advanced project. Maybe more significant, they didn't mind that Elizabeth was a gregarious talker who concentrated more on people than on her needles, and was hardly a model of crafty concentration.

"It took me five months to make those socks," she laughs, "and I never could have done it without that knitting group. I'm way too impatient." She had to rip out her work and restart again and again, but every time the experts in the group guided her through all the tricky steps. It was a learning experience she never could have gotten from a book.

Maybe Elizabeth could have gone a little faster, but she was making a discovery: There was something special about knitting together that—for her at least—made it easier to listen as well as to talk. The clicking needles erased some of the blind-date awkwardness she associated with getting to know people. Silence around the table was okay. And after five months, she had more than two socks to show. She had already made a set of friends good enough to watch trashy TV shows with.

It's a story that seems to be repeating itself almost everywhere there are knitters. People are making connections at knitting circles and meet-ups as far afield as Queens, New York, and Quito, Ecuador. These encounters vary a lot in their scale, atmosphere, and intensity, so interested knitters are advised to try a few and see what fits them best.

Most knitting circles are small groups meeting in private homes or cafés, but those may be relatively difficult to find as a newcomer. The easiest to discover are meet-ups: drop-in sessions at public places—bars, local yarn shops, and more—such as those organized by the dozens of "Stitch 'n Bitch" or "SnB" groups around the USA, or by the Church of Craft, "a nondenominational group of people who love to make stuff," with chapters in nine North American cities and growing. To find one of these groups, ask at your local yarn shop or search on sites like Craftster.org, Craigslist.org, or Knittyboard.com.

The bigger groups typically have a broad mix of skill levels and a real openness to beginners. At a recent Church of Craft meeting in Portland, beginners found seats next to knitters with decades of experience, and were supplied with a mimeographed tutorial, materials, and even coffee and pastries. Eighty or so crafters were splayed around the tables in a big borrowed café, and they ranged from twenty-year-old female boxers to grandmas wearing lilac perfume. It was a vision of casual welcome.

Knitting is so good at hooking up new friends that, especially in big or craft-crazy towns, it's easy for groups to multiply, branch, and spin off into a thousand little variants as relationships develop. As members of public groups start getting together at home, there can be complications worthy of a soap opera.

"I started going to the Seattle Stitch 'n Bitch group once a week," says Jessica Rose, a knitter and blogger from Washington State. "Someone from that group started another group that met on Capitol Hill. I started going to that group, too. Then I started working late on Thursdays at a yarn shop. I invited some friends and customers to join me after work for knitting. That group fluctuated for several months until it boiled down to a group of eight."

That's when it started getting intense. "We became very close. We would get together several times a week for knitting, dinner, coffee. It became a secret group," she says. "We didn't want anyone to come along and crash our party."

The intensity died down after a few members of the secret knitalong group moved away. But Jessica was hooked. She's in five groups now, besides being president of the Seattle Knitters Guild. She recommends the bigger, more anonymous meet-ups for knitters seeking an experience that's free of worrisome social complications.

So why are knitting groups such a powerful friendship machine? "Crafting is something that's very conducive to people bonding," says Sister Diane Gilleland, minister of the Church of Craft in Portland, "because when you're making things, you're very relaxed and you're very positive. It seems to take you outside of the normal social anxieties."

Besides pole-vaulting you past the awkwardness of getting to know new people and placing you in a more receptive zone, some say knitting together taps into the power of creation itself.

Church of Craft founder Callie Janoff suggests that creating things makes us more empathetic to the creations and possibilities of others. "We come together, and we make things, and we affirm the craft we see in each other," she says in one of the Church's few sermons. "Then we go home inspired, confident, peaceful, and we live our lives with all the happiness and love we can."

That's an energy that Elizabeth just couldn't get enough of. Her Sunday knitting group was good, but it wasn't quite sustaining her. She roped together a group of her own, by recruiting her neighbor, someone from an Internet list, and even—gasp—a woman she saw *crocheting* at a bus stop.

The new group met on Friday nights, usually in someone's apartment. They lit candles. They drank wine. The conversation roamed everywhere, from politics to sex to that ultimate in private topics—how much money they really had. They still took their needles, but none of them cared too much about what knitting got accomplished. In short, it was an entirely different atmosphere than the Sunday group.

Elizabeth found she needed both groups to get her fix. Soon enough she had to come clean and tell her Sunday friends about her Friday night adventures. Were they surprised or offended that she was going round town with other knitters?

"Well, there were a few looks," she says. "But mostly I think they were surprised I was interested enough in knitting to start another group, no matter what it was like."

Finding a Knitting Group

Local yarn shops are the best places to learn about local public knitting circles and meet-ups. Many stores host meet-ups themselves. Ask!

The Knitting Guild Association (www.tkga.com) has online message boards and a search function to locate knitting guilds and clubs across the United States.

Stitch 'n Bitch groups and informal meet-ups can be located via **Stitchnbitch.org**, on individual city- and state-level discussion groups at **Yahoogroups.com**, and also under the discussion forums at **www.craftster.org** and **www.knittyboard.com**.

The Church of Craft (www.churchofcraft.org) is not exclusively focused on knitting, but all its meetings are knitter-friendly.

Olive's Afghan

This homage to Larissa's grandmother Olive recalls her many appliance-colored, chevron-patterned creations, but it is updated with a luxurious alpaca/merino blend yarn in slightly less groovy tones. Assembled from eight strips of bias-knit fabric, it can easily be knitted by up to eight people.

FINISHED MEASUREMENTS 66" wide x 60" long (measured from point to point)

YARN Panels: Berroco Ultra Alpaca (50% alpaca / 50% wool; 215 yards / 100 grams): 2 hanks each #6203 Camel Hair, #6284 Prune Mix, #6282 Cranberry Mix, #6238 Medium Orchid, and #6232 Pastel Pink; 3 hanks each #6275 Pea Soup Mix and #6249 Fennel
Finishing: Rowan Classic Yarns Cashsoft Aran (57% extra-fine merino / 33% microfiber / 10% cashmere; 95 yards / 50 grams): 1 ball #15 Sienna (C)

NEEDLES One pair straight needles size US 7 (4.5 mm). Change needle size if necessary to obtain correct gauge.

GAUGE 20 sts and 30 rows = 4" (10 cm) in Garter stitch (knit every row)

NOTES Each Panel requires 2 hanks, 1 each of A and B. The color with which you choose to begin and end each Panel will be color A. The contrasting color in that Panel will be color B. Afghan shown is worked as follows: Panel 1 – A: Fennel, B: Medium Orchid; Panel 2 – A: Camel Hair, B: Prune Mix; Panel 3 – A: Cranberry Mix, B: Pea Soup Mix; Panel 4 – A: Medium Orchid, B: Pastel Pink; Panel 5 – A: Fennel, B: Pea Soup Mix; Panel 6 – A: Fennel, B: Cranberry Mix; Panel 7 – A: Pastel Pink, B: Camel Hair; Panel 8 – A: Pea Soup Mix, B: Prune Mix

AFGHAN

Panel A (make 4)
With A, CO 47 sts.
Row 1: K1, k2tog, knit to last 2 sts, k1-f/b, k1.
Row 2: Knit.
Rows 3-22: Repeat Rows 1 and 2.
Row 23: Change to B. Repeat Row 1.
Rows 24-44: Repeat Rows 2-22. Change to A.
Repeat Rows 1-44 six more times, then repeat Rows 1-21 once (you should have 15 blocks of color). BO all sts.

Panel B (make 4)
With A, CO 47 sts.
Row 1: K1, k1-f/b, knit to last 3 sts, ssk, k1.
Row 2: Knit.
Rows 3-22: Repeat Rows 1 and 2.
Row 23: Change to B. Repeat Row 1.
Rows 24-44: Repeat Rows 2-22.
Repeat Rows 1-44 six more times. Change to A; repeat Rows 1-21 once (you should have 15 blocks of color). BO all sts.

FINISHING

With RS of Panels facing, sew together using whip stitch and C, alternating Panel A and Panel B. *Note: The CO and BO edges of the Panels will form zig-zag edges.* Weave in all ends.

Spectacles and Knit-Ins

You can't experience it on TV. You have to be there to understand. On a good day, a baseball game is a pleasure as subtle and fine—and unknowable to the uninitiated—as running your fingers through pure cashmere.

You settle into your plastic seat while the sun is setting and leave the world outside of the ballpark behind. On the green expanse below, grown men in pinstripes and high socks fidget around a brown dirt track, pause awhile to jabber and point, and occasionally toss a ball. No matter how much trash talk sounds from the stands around you, somehow the stillness of the summer night remains. This is a game with a different, more thoughtful pace. Plus, here, the hot dogs and beer *come to you*.

Just when you think nothing is happening, there's an electric crack: the bat connecting with its target. All eyes rise as the ball arcs up, levels off, and begins its long, fatal fall toward the left field wall. The stadium shudders just a little as ten thousand fans rise to their feet. The outfielder jumps and reaches—but to no avail. The place resounds with cheers, stomping, and the inevitable wave—a little more colorful and hazardous than usual, since everybody in this section has yarn and needles in their hands.

It's Stich N' Pitch night in Seattle, and the nearest thousand or so fans are knitting.

Stitch N' Pitch started modestly in a few West Coast ballparks in 2005, as a promotion like Snow Tire Night or Free Haircut Day. In Seattle, the Mariners were looking to sell more tickets. With knitting's burgeoning popularity, it made sense to try a knitting night. The team's vice president of marketing figured they'd sell 200 tickets—little more than a bunt added to the box-office take. The response was a grand slam—more than 1,200 people showed up. In 2006,

the program was formalized under the sponsorship of The National NeedleArts Association, an organization of fiber-craft businesses, and had firm dates in a dozen or so cities.

Success was no surprise to Nana, a knitter and long-time (and considering their record, oft-suffering) Mariners fan. Live baseball, major or minor league, is a passion for her. She'll sit right behind home plate if she can, studying the game in front of her while listening to another one on her Walkman. "It's important for me to be there when it's happening," she says.

Baseball actually led Nana to take up knitting. She spent so much time watching the game she started looking for things to do with her hands, and tried out crafts. She found the regal pace of the sport, with its long, loping spaces between plays and pitches, was perfect for knitting.

Along the way, she figured out the perfect "ballpark projects." Since seating conditions may be cramped or distracting, she never brings anything too complex or fussy. The game is a good time to knit on large fields of plain Stocki-nette stitch. Projects are best mounted on circular needles, which creates less elbow interaction with neighbors, and which provides extra protection against lost stitches in case you drop something when you're reaching for a hot dog—or, if you get really motivated, a fly ball.

There are more philosophical connections, too. Nana sees baseball as a series of one-on-one match-ups, pitcher versus batter, base stealer versus catcher. When the blistering pitch finally comes, or the runner finally steals for home, ball-players must simply rise to the moment, or not. Skill in base-ball must all happen in a single meditative moment. There's a spirit to it that many knitters are likely to find familiar.

Of course, Stitch N' Pitch is not the only mass meet-up that's been designed expressly for knitters. There have been Stitch 'n Rides on California commuter trains. London's Cast Off: The Knitting Club for Boys and Girls occasionally takes over a subway car or a movie matinee (negotiating to get the house lights left on so they can see their work). Cast Off even orchestrated a wedding in which everything—the bride's dress, the cake, the corsage, and the presents—were knitted (see page 116).

The widest spectacle, though a bit harder to notice than a knitted wedding procession, might be World Wide Knit in Public Day, coordinated over the Internet by Australian "sheep geek" Danielle Landes. In 2006, she says, more than 4,000 knitters in seventeen different countries gathered locally in public spots to knit. For most participants, it's all in the spirit of celebration and solidarity, a common interest that can bring disparate people together.

"We're all knitters, no matter what else we may be," writes Danielle. "That's more than enough to spark a conversation."

But for some knitters, knitalongs like the Knit in Public Day are more than simple parties. They offer a forum for "coming out" as crafters. Some artists and academic types feel craft is dismissed because it's not art. Other people fear knitting is too feminine, too old-fashioned, or even in some places, too hip and faddish. Others are tired of constantly having to answer the question, "What are you doing?"

"I think there are many shy knitters out there. I used to be one of them," says Danielle. "Drawing attention to myself from strangers while knitting was something worth avoiding." Organizing World Wide Knit in Public Day

Knitting Spectacles

Stitch N' Pitch
A program of The National
NeedleArts Association.
www.stitchnpitch.com

**World Wide Knit
in Public Day**
Informally coordinated
by Danielle Landes.
www.wwkipday.com

**Cast Off: The Knitting Club
for Boys and Girls**
www.castoff.info

helped her stop hiding her knitting, and she hopes it will help others, too.

Other knitters have equally strong emotions, and use public knitalongs to voice them.

"This is a way of saying, 'I knit, and I'm not ashamed,'" one movie-matinee knitter told the *London Times*.

"One reason I knit on the bus," says Melissa, a defiant knitter who accompanied baseball diehard Nana to the Mariners Stitch N' Pitch event, "is I want people to know that's the way I value my time. They'll be dumbfounded that I'm knitting a pair of socks. I'll say yes, I am. Making things is important to me, and I want people to know it."

More power to you, Melissa. Now if the batter could only take a swing with that kind of attitude. . . .

A knitalong saved me when I was sentenced to six weeks in bed.

It was spring, I was pregnant with my first baby, and I had been put on bed rest. The view from my pillow consisted mostly of my dog's snout, prodding me endlessly to go out, wondering why the household walk-in-the-park policy had suddenly changed.

I found refuge in an ingenious pattern by Genia Planck, the Pinwheel Baby Blanket. I started making one as a present for Truman—the soon-to-be-born son of a pregnant friend, due just two weeks before my baby. Since the round shape and spiral design reminded me of the shapes and animals I had seen in a tide pool on the Oregon coast, I modeled the colors of Truman's blanket on a tide pool, too—and dreamed up a picot edging of vivid green tendrils to magnify the sea-anemone effect.

Halfway through Truman's blanket, my curiosity about the pattern was already turning to obsession.

You know the feeling, when you're not even 60 percent done with something, and already you're dreaming of the next, and the next. That was me and the pinwheel.

Some of my fellow knit bloggers were making pinwheels, too, and they all looked so different. A simple change in materials or color could give the piece an entirely different feel. A twist of the blocking pins could turn it from a pizza into a ten-point star. I could hardly wait to get started with a dozen different adaptations.

In the meantime, I used my blog to start the most informal knitalong imaginable.

"I'm still so into this blankie pattern, and the stunning results," I wrote to anyone who happened to stop by, "I decided to start a gallery & knitalong page. It has a few tips, a link to the free pattern, border ideas, and hopefully inspirational pictures. Please let me know if you are working on a pinwheel blanket by commenting below or e-mailing me. Even if you are not finished yet, I'll link to your progress and then your finished blanket when the time comes."

That was it—just an invitation to knit with me, and a page or two on the Internet to share pictures

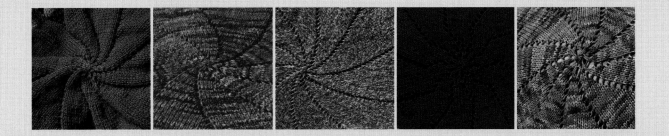

and tips. No deadlines or prizes or databases. No complications.

Over the next few months, I started a pinwheel blanket for my own baby, and my gallery of pictures grew as more and more people signed up. I wrote tips on how to start a pinwheel (a tricky beginning maneuver for an otherwise super-simple project), and I created and posted a little Excel spreadsheet that predicted one's blanket's diameter based on gauge and stitch count.

Soon more than four dozen blanket photographs (and one ravenous baby boy) had arrived in my life, and so I shifted the pictures off my personal blog and onto a public photo-sharing site called Flickr.com, so participants could post their own pinwheels without me having to handle the pictures.

But no matter which website hosted it, the gallery was a wondrous variety of expressions—swirls of earthy cotton, targets in wild fluorescent colors, puddles of wool, mottled and inviting. I was so enamored with the results, I started giving other knitters' blankets nicknames. Deedee's Burnt Autumn, Abigail's Sweet Tart Target. One red, white, and blue favorite of mine, made by a knitter named Abby, looked just like a Bomb Pop ice cream novelty. I was amazed at what different knitters could do with the same basic pattern. Every new picture was a revelation.

I've had a special interest in knitalongs ever since then. That pinwheel gallery convinced me that knitalongs have a lot to teach knitters on every level, about the possibilities of color and form, about the way knitters' personalities get imbued in their handiwork, whether they intend it or not, and about what a gift it is to find a "pure pattern"—one that is simple and elegant and open to endless possibility.

I still like looking at the pinwheel gallery, a small sampling of which is reproduced here. I hope you'll visit the whole group at Knitalong.net, and add to it by making your own little spiral masterpiece.

1. Chris O'Brien, St. Louis, MO 2. Cara Conomos Davis, Secaucus, NJ 3. Chawne Kimber, Easton, PA 4. Rebecca Hunt, Boston, MA 5. Jennifer C. Kogut, Seattle, WA 6. Chawne Kimber, Easton, PA 7. Kyrie Mead, Corvallis, OR 8. NoellesNoodles.com, Albuquerque, NM 9. Kelly Sue DeConnick, Kansas City, MO 10. Sheree O'Brien, Aliso Viejo, CA

Pinwheel Blanket

Baseballs are round. Babies are round (or at least rounded). And one of the most mesmerizing knitting patterns ever is round, too. The Pinwheel Blanket is a scrumptious pizza of a baby blanket, knit from the center out with any kind of yarn and any appropriately-sized needles. The pinwheel is perhaps the most perfect knitalong project imaginable. It's simple and elegant, is totally flexible, allows for creativity within structure, is easy to knit even among chatty company, and showcases an endless range of gorgeous variegated or mottled yarns through its total lack of cables, bumps, or other infringing irregularities. DESIGN BY GENIA PLANCK

FINISHED MEASUREMENTS 113" circumference, 36" diameter

YARN Classic Elite Yarns Waterlily (100% extra-fine merino; 100 yards / 50 grams): 7 balls #1927 Bramble

NEEDLES One set of five double-pointed needles (dpn) size US 7 (4.5 mm)
One 24" (60 cm) or 29" (75 cm) circular needle (circ) size US 7 (4.5 mm).
Change needle size if necessary to obtain correct gauge.

NOTIONS Stitch markers

GAUGE 16 sts and 22 rows = 4" (10 cm) in Stockinette stitch (St st)

BLANKET

Note: Change to circ needle when necessary for number of sts on needles.

With dpn, CO 5 sts, divide among 4 needles. Join for working in the rnd, being careful not to twist sts; place marker (pm) for beginning of rnd.

Rnd 1 and Every Other Odd-Numbered Rnd: Knit.
Rnd 2: *K1-f/b; repeat from * around–10 sts.
Rnd 4: *K1, yo, pm; repeat from * to last st, k1, yo–20 sts.
Rnd 6: *Knit to marker, yo, slip marker (sm); repeat from * around–30 sts.

Repeat Rnd 6 every other rnd until you have 430 sts [43 sts between markers], ending with an odd-numbered rnd.

Seed Stitch Border

Rnd 1: *K1, p1; repeat from * around.
Rnd 2: Knitting the purl sts, and purling the knit sts as they face you, *work to marker, sm, yo; repeat from * around–440 sts [44 sts between markers].
Rnd 3: Knit the purl sts and purl the knit sts as they face you, working the increased sts in Seed st.
Rnd 4: Repeat Rnd 2–450 sts [45 sts between markers]. BO all sts loosely in pattern.

FINISHING

Block Blanket. *Note: You may block the Blanket so that it is circular, or so that the points form a 10-pointed pinwheel shape.*

Chapter Two Remembering

Knitting bees, meet-ups, and knit cafés are a great source of companionship for knitters today. But for some, the camaraderie they feel isn't just with people across the table.

Knitting together helps them tap into the experiences of their grandparents' lives, and *their* grandparents' lives too—back to times when making things with your hands was a central part of everyday life.

The craft has "definitely brought me a little closer to my grandma," writes a knit blogger named Madalyn, who's come to understand her grandmother's slightly obsessive pattern of knitting, finishing, ripping, and knitting things up again.

Back before grandma's first stitch, there were times and places when knitting together was even more common than it is now. In certain decades of the 1700s and 1800s, knitting was ever-present in many English and Scottish villages and rural towns across America.

Most females, and not a few boys, were knitters to some extent, and often enough that they took their knitting with them all day long: to the pasture to check on the livestock, to town on a market day, to the houses of friends and neighbors on visits (which was irreplaceable socializing in the days before phones and e-mail). "The knitting-needles and the worsted are continually in their hands," wrote a traveler about women in Scotland's Shetland Islands, "and seem to form part and parcel of the woman herself." When these women got together, the needles came out as a matter of course, though no one would have used the word *knitalong*.

There's at least one difference between those experiences and the knitalongs you can join today: Those people weren't knitting just because it was a wonderful creative experience. They were working—sometimes for money, sometimes to clothe their families, and sometimes because they felt compelled to knit by forces far beyond their control. They knitted together partly to make that hard work easier to bear.

In this chapter, we revisit three kinds of knitalongs from the past, where knitting together was a reaction to difficult times, and maybe even a source of hope.

First we remember hand-knitting as piecework in a cottage industry for textiles. There are still thousands who do this today in places like India, Madagascar, and China, hand-knitting designer garments for sale elsewhere (the ease of global trade means that some Indian hand-knitting brokers sell classic Irish Aran garments). But in North America and Western Europe, hand-knitting as a significant industry only lasted until the 1800s. We revisit hand-knitting operations in the Dales of England and the American frontier, where knitters sang, held contests, and generally did everything in their power to ease themselves through the difficulty and weariness of piecework. Since those knitters worked most often on stockings, we pair that story with Socks 101, a pattern and knitalong designed to ease today's knitters through their first pair of socks.

As machine and factory knitting took over the production of basic garments like socks and hats, hand-knitting hung on as a domestic craft with virtuous overtones. If you were knitting, you probably weren't getting into much trouble. That made it a frequently recommended activity for people whom society said could be tempted to sin out of "idleness," from homeless single women in the Boston Female Asylum to the converts of missionaries in Hawaii. We revisit a school where orphans sat together to knit miniature novelties and elaborate lacework pieces, for show and for institutional fund-raising—a story that inspired our lacy Victorian Baby Bonnet.

The biggest knitalongs in history were brought on by war. Many knitters have heard about Red Cross knitting drives and the knitting work of luminaries like Eleanor Roosevelt, who churned out socks, hats, and gloves to warm and comfort men in the field. Our war story looks at how women on *both* sides of the battle lines knit for their men, and compares those scenes to current wartime knitalongs. In one, crafters inspired by a Japanese legend are knitting a prayer for peace in the form of a thousand felted cranes. With the Felted Peace Crane pattern we provide, you can make one of your own to add to the prayer.

For most of us, knitting is no longer compulsory work, and the togetherness we get from knitting along is more about celebration than relief. But knowing the meaning of knitting for our ancestors can give us a deeper appreciation of every stitch.

Knitting as a Cottage Industry

In the picturesque English valley of Dentdale, smack in the middle of sheep country, there were certain times of the year practically everyone—men, women, and children, with infants and vicars as the only likely exceptions—could be seen knitting. They knitted in huts, on carts, and under bridges. It was the local obsession in the late 1700s.

As the sun set, people gathered for a "sitting"—an evening of knitting and diversion. In fits and starts, several families arrived, crowding into a small cottage. They took seats around the room and began to knit in the fire- and candlelight. They didn't look like today's knitters—some of them rocked back and forth as they knit with the help of "sheaths" stuck in their belts. Feet tapped on the floor. Soon someone began singing, a song to help count the rounds of stockings in progress—a song that seems, naturally enough, to be about a sheep named Bell and a fran-tic sheepdog named Rockie. While they each knitted one round of stocking, they sang:

> Bell—wether o Barking, cries Baa, baa,
> How many sheep have we lost to-day?
> Nineteen we have lost, one have we fun,
> Run Rockie, run Rockie, run, run, run.

For the next round, they adjusted the number down:

> Bell—wether o Barking, cries Baa, baa,
> How many sheep have we lost to-day?
> Eighteen we have lost, one have we fun,
> Run Rockie, run Rockie, run, run, run.

They continued until that section of everyone's stocking was done.

An upper-class observer of one such sitting was impressed. "Beautiful gloves were thrown off complete, and worsted stockings made good progress," he wrote. But he was even more charmed by the way the knitters entertained themselves.

"No one could foretell the current of the evening's talk. They had their ghost tales, and their love tales, and their battles of jests and riddles, and their ancient tales of enormous length." Sometimes for a change they had someone read, for example, from Robinson Crusoe. "No sound was heard but the reader's voice and the click of the knitting needles," the writer recollects.

Dentdale sounds straight-out romantic in this account from Richard Rutt's book *A History of Hand Knitting* (the song is from *The Old Hand-Knitters of the Dales* by Marie Hartley and Joan Ingilby). But Rutt's book has another description of Dentdale as well. An eight-year-old named Betty Yewdale was sent by her parents to Dent to learn to knit. Betty found that new career trying. She was constantly knitting, at school and in her new home. There were songs and games, but the point of them was to try to make Betty and everyone else knit faster and faster. Four yarns were wound up in a single ball, to make four children race. They knit from it all at once, with the slowest knitters tangling the whole thing up.

It was a lot of pressure for an eight-year-old. Betty escaped and walked thirty miles home through the snow. She'd had it with knitting school. Her parents seem to have accepted the decision and not sent her back.

Dentdale was obsessed with knitting because there, it wasn't just a pastime. It was the local industry, and people knitted items to sell for money—socks and garments that would eventually end up on the bodies of customers around the country and the world. It was a piecework job; they got paid by the finished item, not by the hour. The incentive was to knit as much as possible, and the "sittings" and games were there to help relieve the drudgery, and maybe even the physical pain, of knitting hard and long.

It's tough to imagine that world now, when you can buy a ten-pack of factory-made socks for a few dollars, but this was a time when the vast majority of socks, stockings, and gloves in the Western world were not just knitted, but knitted by hand. They were *knitted* because knitted fabric has properties of stretch, shapability, and seamlessness that make it superior to woven and sewn work for those garments. They were knitted *by hand* because knitting machines, though in existence from the 1600s, took centuries to overtake hand production. And they were knitted in the countryside because wool was plentiful there and better jobs were not.

In the British Isles, production took up a systematic, commercial form in several places like Dentdale, Wensleydale, and the Shetland Islands. In America, the need for hand-knitted garments was similar, but the frontier expansion of the country made the hand-knitting industry more

variable, and less of a trap. One classic image, repeated in dozens if not hundreds of stories about eighteenth- and nineteenth-century frontier homesteads, has a visitor opening the door to a cabin and finding the family—Grandma, Ma, all the sisters, and even the little brother—all at their handiwork by the fire.

Before the Civil War, a lot of rural families were engaged in a continual low-level knitalong. Kids learned so early that many women couldn't remember a time when they *didn't* know how to knit.

"At six years of age, I was already knitting my own stocking without assistance in heel and toe," bragged Mary Farnsworth, born in Connecticut in 1830, in her handwritten autobiography. She was clearly proud of what she could do. But she probably would have had to knit even if she didn't like it. Some families had a quota that girls and boys needed to finish each day—an inch of sock, or even half a sock.

Much of the time, the socks, mittens, and hats they made were for their own family's consumption. But piecework knitting was something people could do on their own schedule, and therefore an opportunity for anybody who needed extra cash. Sales were made to neighbors or to local shopkeepers. The pay wasn't great. Women in the Pacific Northwest in the mid-1800s were getting about fifty cents per pair of socks, and they could perhaps knit one man's sock per night, to be resold to miners and fishermen. It was pay that kept "the wolf from the door," said a Washington State settler named Mary Ellen Todd, quoted in Anne Macdonald's *No Idle Hands*. But the security was hard-earned by relentless knitting every single night.

Economic necessity didn't stop people from using knitting to socialize. In more sparsely populated areas of the countryside, the hardest fiber chores, like cleaning wool, were great excuses for women to travel away from home and get together. For women who hadn't seen another adult female in weeks or months, those trips could be inviolable holidays. There were bees, too, to finish the knitting needed for the upcoming winter.

Among the women who worked hard at knitting, there were of course some natural enthusiasts. Beyond the country and frontier settings, younger and more energetic "townies" took their needles around practically everywhere, and produced garments even as they gossiped.

"After I was married and the children were growing up, I was never without a pair of needles in my hands," reminisced Elizabeth E. Miller, born in 1848 in South Ryegate, Vermont, when she was interviewed by a government folklorist at ninety years of age. "When I went out to a sociable or a farmer's meeting in the evening I always took my knitting. We had a spanking pair [of horses] then and when we were out in the [wagon] I knit up hill and down . . . my knitting went everywhere but to church."

Elizabeth Miller loved knitting as much as any fiber enthusiast today. Her kind of knitting signaled the coming of a new breed of knitter that is most familiar today—the knitter who does it because he or she wants to, and simply can't bear to stop.

For those in the nineteenth century who didn't love knitting as much as Elizabeth, it eventually became less compulsory. When it became possible to say "no" to knitting, perhaps because of new wealth, the availability of cheap machine-made items, or simply because knitters were bold enough to make their own decisions, a lot of them did so—just like little Betty Yewdale back in Dent.

By the late 1800s, most of the women carrying knitting around in their pockets and bags were doing so because they wanted to—not because they had to. Which, we can all agree, is just how it should be.

Recommended Reading

....

A History of Hand Knitting by Richard Rutt
(Interweave Press, 1987)

The Old Hand-Knitters of the Dales
by Marie Hartley and Joan Ingilby
(Dalesman, 1951, 1969, 2001)

*Knitting America: A Glorious Heritage
from Warm Socks to High Art*
by Susan M. Strawn
(Voyageur Press, 2007)

*No Idle Hands: A Social History
of American Knitting*
by Anne L. Macdonald
(Ballantine Books, 1988)

American Memory at the
Library of Congress,
memory.loc.gov/ammem
This is a huge free database that may be
searched for texts and accounts of
American life, including knitting.

larissa's

SOCKS 101

Knitalong Diary

One day my friend Kim wanted to make a sock.

Kim is one of my best knitalong companions, always inspiring me (and maddeningly, always loving the *exact* same yarns and colors I do). Knitting since childhood, she had made beautiful sweaters and scarves, but she found sock knitting mysterious. Kim's mother threw off pairs of socks on size 1 needles like she was putting away shots of whiskey. But Kim had yet to learn.

Hand-knit socks really do feel sumptuous and they offer the knitter a special sense of accomplishment and ineffable joy. But many skilled knitters are put off by the unknowns of sock-making. Just like Kim, they might knit for years and never turn a heel, even though they're intrigued.

That would have been impossible in the past. People used to knit a *lot* of socks. A *heck* of a lot of socks: coarse socks, fine socks, warm socks, and (according to one traveler to the Shetland Islands) long stockings so fine and limpid you could pull them through a wedding band. Before 1900 you could hardly *be* a knitter and not work on "hose." If you were knitting with other people, in all likelihood at least one of you would be working on a foot.

So the day Kim confessed she wanted to make a sock, I must have felt it was my historic duty. I set out, with her in tow, to create a sock. One so fun, on such big needles, and with such an indulgent yarn, she could not fail. A sock so fast I could walk her through cast on, cuff, heel, and gusset in one sitting. The kind of sock that starts out "cast on 32 stitches." A learning sock, but one absolutely worth keeping when the lesson was through.

Recreating that sock for a book about knitting together just made sense. It would ease the beginner's dilemma—how to learn sock-making, when so much of it is most easily learned *from other knitters.*

But would it work? I hosted a knitalong to see how the Socks 101 pattern fared.

As with most of my knitalongs, it started impulsively with a quick invitation on a blog I created. Anyone who signed up got a password to view the pattern.

Joiners could discuss the pattern with blog comments, and a photo-sharing website helped everyone display pictures of their progress. I set a deadline that was inspirationally close and said "Go!"

Soon we were trading tips just like old-fashioned frontier women around a virtual hearth.

"Hello, brand new sock knitter here," wrote Moody Mama. "I'm wondering how I can achieve the nice rounded toe I am seeing on all of these lovely socks. My first one ended up with kind of a pointy square toe."

"The toe gets rounded by pulling the Kitchener stitch fairly snug on the two stitches furthest to the outside," I opined, hoping that would help.

"*Knitty* has a nice tutorial on the Kitchener," chimed in Koocheekoo with a link.

The give and take of chatter like this was all some knitters needed, and soon our knitalong had produced about 50 pairs of simple, toasty ankle socks—more than a few of them created by first-timers.

"I'm almost finished with my first sock ever!" enthused Cindy. "A picture of the work so far is on my blog. This is fun." Mama Urchin wrote, "I'm still amazed that I knit a pair of socks," and vowed she'd make more in the future.

Like Kim and I, these knitters worked together and discovered a new addictive joy. "My first socks ever! They were so fast to knit that I hardly had time to feel intimidated. Now I'm feeling obnoxiously over-confident," joked Shoeless Val.

Thanks to a knitalong, she was connected to hundreds of years of knitting sisterhood—and though she may call herself "shoeless" on the Internet, she is shy about socks no more.

1. Michelle Schwengel-Regala, O'ahu, HI 2. Valerie Wallis, Logan, UT 3. Maryse Roudier, Milford, MA 4. Amanda Jenkins, Santa Cruz, CA 5. Carrie Workman, Auburn, WA 6. Carin Glick, Manchester, NH 7. Lia Harris, McMinnville, OR 8. Sarah Gilbert, Portland, OR 9. Chawne Kimber, Easton, PA 10. Cheryl Killingsworth, Roland, AR

Socks 101

Warm, well-fitting handmade socks used to be essential for warmth and survival, or, if you could knit fast enough, they were the source of a few extra coins. Today, the stakes aren't quite so high; they are mostly made for comfort and for the challenge and pleasure of knitting them. Knitting a pair of socks for the first time is a defining moment—a graduation of sorts. Many knitters don't get through their first pair without at least a little help from a teacher or friend. These socks have that two-person knitalong experience in mind. They're designed to be quick, so one knitter can sit down with another and navigate the pattern together.

SIZES Women's Small (Women's Medium, Women's Large/Men's Small, Men's Medium)
Shown in size Women's Medium

FINISHED MEASUREMENTS Circumference at ball of foot: 7 (8, 9, 10)"

YARN Manos del Uruguay Wool (100% wool; 138 yards / 100 grams): 1 (1, 2, 2) skeins #24 Blush

NEEDLES One set of five double-pointed needles (dpn) size US 10 (6 mm). Change needle size if necessary to obtain correct gauge.

NOTIONS Stitch marker

GAUGE 16 sts and 22 rnds = 4" (10 cm) in Stockinette stitch (St st)

NOTES
The pattern is written for a set of 5 dpns, and at times it notes how many stitches are on each needle. If you use 4 dpns or work on circular needles instead, disregard the needle- and stitch-shifting instructions.

2x2 Rib
(multiple of 4 sts; 1-rnd repeat)
All Rnds: *K2, p2; repeat from * around.

SOCKS (MAKE 2)
Cuff
CO 28 (32, 36, 40) sts, divide among 3 needles as follows:
Needle 1: 8 (8, 10, 10) sts; **Needle 2:** 12 (16, 16, 20) sts; **Needle 3:** 8 (8, 10, 10) sts. Join for working in the rnd, being careful not to twist sts; place marker (pm) for beginning of rnd. Begin 2x2 Rib. Work even for 6 (6, 8, 8) rounds.
Next Rnd: Change to St st (knit every rnd). Work even for 2 rnds. Redistribute sts as follows: **Needle 1:** 7 (8, 9, 10) sts; **Needle 2:** 14 (16, 18, 20) sts; **Needle 3:** 7 (8, 9, 10) sts. Remove marker.

Heel Flap
Note: Slip all sts purlwise.
Knit across Needle 1. Knit across Needle 2. Turn work, ready to work back and forth on 14 (16, 18, 20) sts on Needle 2 only. Needles 1 and 3 will remain out of work while you work the Heel Flap.
Row 1 (WS): Slip 1, purl to end of needle.
Row 2: Slip 1, knit to end of needle. Repeat Rows 1 and 2 until Heel Flap measures 2¼ (2¼, 3, 3)" [approximately 12 (12, 16, 16) rows], ending with a WS row.

Turn Heel
Set-Up Row 1 (RS): Slip 1, k8 (10, 10, 12), ssk, k1, turn.
Set-Up Row 2: Slip 1, p5 (7, 5, 7), p2tog, p1, turn.
Row 1: Slip 1, knit to 1 st before gap, ssk (bringing together

the 2 sts on either side of gap), k1, turn.

Row 2: Slip 1, purl to 1 st before gap, p2tog (the 2 sts on either side of gap), p1, turn.

Repeat Rows 1 and 2 zero (one, one, two) more times, omitting the final k1 and p1 sts in the last repeat of Rows 1 and 2 for sizes Women's Medium and Men's Medium–10 (10, 12, 12) sts remain.

Next Row: Slip 1, knit to end; do NOT turn.

Heel Gusset

With new needle, pick up and knit sts along first side of Heel Flap, picking up 1 st for each slipped edge st, plus one or two more to bridge the gap to the Instep.

With a separate needle, knit all sts from Needles 3 and 1 onto a single needle. This is now your Instep needle.

With a separate needle, pick up and knit sts along second side of Heel Flap, being sure to pick up the same number as on left side of Heel Flap. Knit half the Heel sts onto this same needle.

Transfer the remaining Heel sts to the left-side needle, being careful not to twist them. You are now back to working on 3 needles: **Needle 1:** Left-side needle; **Needle 2:** Instep needle [14 (16, 18, 20) sts]; **Needle 3:** Right-side needle with same number of sts as Left-side needle. Your working yarn is currently at the back center Heel. Place marker for new beginning of rnd.

Decrease Rnd: Needle1, knit to last 3 sts, k2tog, k1; Needle 2, knit; Needle 3, k1, ssk, knit to end.

Next Rnd: Knit.

Repeat last 2 rnds until 7 (8, 9, 10) sts remain on Needles 1 and 3–28 (32, 36, 40) sts total. *Note: Number of sts on Needle 2 will not change.*

Foot

Work even in St st until Foot measures 7 (7^1/$_2$, 8^1/$_2$, 9^1/$_4$)" from back of Heel, or to 2" less than desired finished length.

Toe

Rnd 1: Needle 1, knit to last 3 sts, k2tog, k1; Needle 2, k1, ssk, knit to last 3 sts, k2tog, k1; Needle 3, k1, ssk, knit to end–24 (28, 32, 36) sts remain.

Next Rnd: Knit.

Repeat last 2 rnds 4 (5, 5, 6) times–8 (8, 12, 12) sts remain. K2 (2, 3, 3) from Needle 1 onto Needle 3. *Note: You should now have the same number of sts on Needles 2 and 3.* Cut yarn, leaving a 10" tail. Graft sts together using Kitchener Stitch (see page 156).

FINISHING

Weave in all ends. Full the socks as follows: Dampen under cold running water; do NOT soak. Run through a preheated clothes dryer on high (cotton) setting for 5 minutes, or for length of time desired to achieve springy, stretchy, not limp fabric. This may take longer than 5 minutes; check the socks every 5 minutes to ensure you do not over-full them.

Knitting as Character Reform

It was a completely silent knitalong, reserved even by the straight-laced standards of 1834.

The scene was the Pennsylvania Institution, a plain saltbox building on Market Street in Philadelphia. On the upper floor, in a room crammed with odd machines, a model locomotive ran round. It was chased with excitement by a little boy, but he never cried out or laughed once. The only sound was the stomp and patter of his feet.

Next door, in a classroom, girls in drapelike winter dresses sat in rows, manipulating threads and tiny slices of straw with tools no thicker than pins. They were knitting and embroidering clothes and hats for dolls. One small girl turned to show off the fruits of her labor: a glove, perfectly proportioned, no bigger than a thumbnail.

"Brother! Georgie!" she said nonsensically, and smiled. These were the two words she had learned before going deaf and mute—like everyone else in the building. The deaf girls were knitting together because it was part of their curriculum, and because the things they made sold at charity fund-raisers.

In the eighteenth and nineteenth centuries in America and England, many institutions serving "troubled" populations—from the orphans at New York's Asylum for Friendless Boys, to the patients of the Massachusetts Lunatic Asylum, to the single women at the Boston Female Asylum—had knitting programs.

It made sense at the time. Knitting was considered a valuable form of freelance employment (see "Knitting as a Cottage Industry" on page 42), and teaching people how to knit was touted widely as an economic empowerment program.

"WANTED, a MISTRESS, for the Green Cod Charity School, Camberwell-green," read an ad in the *Times of London*. "She must not be under 28 nor above 40 years of age, and of the Church of England; must have a perfect knowledge of knitting stockings." The idea was to give orphans a skill that would give them better employment opportunities as servants.

"The knitting of stockings deserves the greatest encouragement," gushed a columnist for a Philadelphia magazine called *The American Museum* in 1788. "It peculiarly recommends itself by its great utility to the poor . . . It may be performed when walking about the streets, or when confined to a sick room, and by persons blind, lame, or bed-ridden . . . Women, after a day's labor in the field, may work at it without any fatigue, until they go to rest."

It seems doubtful that this writer followed this work regimen himself, or that large numbers of people lifted themselves out of poverty by knitting socks. But the writer's ideas were popular, because knitting wasn't just work, it was a highly moral activity. It kept the knitter from falling idle and getting exposed to a smorgasbord of temptations.

"*No Time is allowed for Idleness or Play*," read the schedule promoted by one Georgia orphanage in 1741. Idle hours were "*Satan's darling Hours to tempt Children to all Manner of Wickedness*, as Lying, Cursing, Swearing, Uncleanness, &c." To keep children virtuous, the day included four hours of school, five hours of prayer and "exhortation," and four hours of work—which for many was knitting. The orphans probably knitted stockings for themselves, and more for the orphanage to sell.

Over the next century, knitting became part of missionary work, too. Christians proclaiming the gospel of Jesus in "heathen nations" also proclaimed a lesser gospel of work and busyness. Knitting was part of that industrious ethic. Missionaries wrote home to their sponsors in England and America about it with pride:

"The people become more industrious. The knitting-school flourishes," wrote a missionary in South Africa in 1811.

"They are taught the preciousness of time," wrote the mistress of a girls' mission school in Persia in 1841, "and fill up the moments . . . in reading, knitting, or other labor which may benefit themselves or others."

Back in America, knitting in institutions was slowly changing. From the mid-1800s to World War I, orphanages, homes for the blind, and asylums still had their charges knit things for sale, but the focus was less on commodities like plain socks and more on novelties and fancy work: toys, doll clothes, and elaborate bonnets and counterpanes (bedspreads). These were the kinds of patterns upper-class hobby knitters admired.

There was also a growing recognition of knitting as psychological instead of religious therapy. As early as 1838, a psychologist named Pliny Earle recommended "useful activity," specifically knitting, as a calming influence for mental health patients. The *New Haven Courier* wrote about a violent lunatic who sat subdued in bed, letting his mother take care of him, as long as he had his yarn and needles. (His mom had chained him to the floor just in case he dropped them and lost his cool.) Asylum and hospital managers regularly promoted the craftiness of the patients. In World War I, wounded soldiers were taught to knit as part of their convalescence.

"The purpose is deeper than merely providing one way to relax," summed up a *New York Times* reporter in 1935. "The psychological factors underlying it all are recognized by psychiatrists . . . it is a way to build, to create something; a foothold in reality for the patient who is groping about in fantasy and illusion."

It's an explanation that seems strangely apropos today, no matter one's state of mental health. Knitting is so renowned for its stress-relieving qualities it's been dubbed "the new yoga." Though formal modern scientific evidence about knitting is sparse, there are hundreds of anecdotes about the grounding effects of the craft, from senior citizens, children with autism, pregnant women, the incarcerated, and the merely stressed out ("Knitting Is My Prozac" was the title for one essay in the zine *Cement Teepee*).

Databases like these, typically available in libraries, are mines of knitting lore.

- *New York Times historical*
- *The Times of London historical*
- *The American Periodical Series*

The craft still has a place in today's "welfare" institutions, though it's no longer the required activity it could have been two centuries ago. Heather Rebmann, a social worker in Boston, started an informal knitting group at a home for troubled teen moms, but only after the moms themselves bugged her to start it. In an essay in the journal *Social Work with Groups*, Heather describes how learning to knit, and helping others to knit, was a way her clients could experience calm, take risks, and feel empowered by the process of creating. One threatening and standoffish twenty-year-old named Sheila was transformed.

"I'm mad calm," Sheila said as she started knitting. "I'm focused." And as the needles clicked, she finally opened up to Heather—not about her anger, but about her dreams.

Victorian Baby Bonnet

Victorian knitting programs for orphans, the disabled, and other causes often resulted in fancy work that could raise funds at charity auctions. This beribboned infant bonnet is inspired by that sort of knitting, though this project is hardly compulsory. Instead, we hope you will enjoy indulging in this updated version, knit with thicker yarn than yesteryear's bonnets.

SIZES One size; fits newborn to 6 months

FINISHED MEASUREMENTS 13¹/₂" from neck edge to neck edge, over top of head

YARN Tahki Yarns Cotton Classic (100% mercerized cotton; 108 yards / 50 grams): 1 hank each #3752 Sage (MC) and #3358 Rust (A)

NEEDLES One circular needle size US 6 (4 mm), any length. Change needle size if necessary to obtain correct gauge.

NOTIONS Stitch holder; 1 yard ³/₈" wide satin ribbon

GAUGE 20 sts and 24 rows = 4" (10 cm) in Stockinette stitch (St st)

BONNET

With Long-Tail CO (see page 156) and A, CO 59 sts. Knit 1 row. Cut yarn, leaving a 5" tail.

BEGIN PATTERN

Row 1 (RS): Change to MC; knit.
Rows 2 and 4: K2, purl to last 2 sts, k2.
Row 3: K3, *[yo, k1] 3 times, [ssk] twice, dcd, [k2tog] twice, [k1, yo] 3 times, k1; repeat from * to last 2 sts, k2.
Rows 5-36: Repeat Rows 1-4.

SHAPE BONNET

Row 37: Knit.
Rows 38, 40, 42, 44, and 46: Repeat Row 2.

Row 39: K3, *yo, k1, yo, k2, [ssk] twice, dcd, [k2tog] twice, k2, [yo, k1] twice; repeat from * to last 2 sts, k2–53 sts remain.
Row 41: K3, *yo, k2, [ssk] twice, dcd, [k2tog] twice, k2, yo, k1; repeat from * to last 2 sts, k2–41 sts remain.
Row 43: K3, *[ssk] twice, dcd, [k2tog] twice, k1; repeat from * to last 2 sts, k2–23 sts remain.
Row 45: K2, ssk, dcd, k2tog, k1, dcd, k2tog, k1, dcd, k2tog, k2–13 sts remain.
Row 47: K2, *dcd; repeat from * to last 2 sts, k2–7 sts remain.
Transfer sts to stitch holder; cut yarn, leaving a 6" tail.

FINISHING

Neck Edging: With RS facing, beginning just after CO edge, with MC, pick up and knit 23 sts along right side of piece to st holder, work across 7 sts from holder, pick up and knit 23 sts along left side of piece to just before CO edge–53 sts.
Rows 1 (WS) and 2: Knit.
Row 3: K2, purl to last 2 sts, k2.
Row 4: K2, [yo, k2tog, k2] 3 times, [yo, k2tog, k1] 4 times, k1 (center back st), [k1, k2tog, yo] 4 times, [k2, k2tog, yo] 3 times, k2.
Row 5: Repeat Row 3.
Row 6: Knit.
BO all sts knitwise.

Weave in all ends, and block piece if desired. Thread ribbon through eyelets as shown.

Knitting in War and Peace

World War I was heading into its first miserable winter, and on both sides of the trenches, women were knitting along.

From Paris, a *New York Times* correspondent wrote that the fashionable set of the City of Lights would not be conquered by the reality of the war! Even as their elegant cars were commandeered by the army, even as khaki uniforms took the place of their satin gowns at Maxim's, the tarts and dandies still promenaded the Champs Elysées. They still sat in chairs under trees and gazed out, to see and be seen.

Then, with the first breath of cold fall air, their eyes turned downward. "One can now see them in scores, sitting under the trees busily bending over their hands, for they are knitting," the reporter wrote. "All feminine Paris is knitting."

Meanwhile in Berlin, capital of rival Germany, a photographer captured eerily similar scenes. One shows prim women in an elegant drawing room, knitting in the company of a well-dressed officer. Another shows a sea of women knitting together—young, old, large, tiny, lovely, plain, some in elaborately embroidered peasant dress.

Friend and foe were making the same things, for the same reasons. The socks, shirts, and mufflers were for the men who were in the mud and cold of the trenches, and the goal was to provide a sliver of warmth and comfort, maybe enough to make a difference between life and death for the soldiers, and hope and despair for all.

Knitting has long been part of war. For centuries, warm hand-knit items were as essential as rifles and bullets. Certain garments, like socks and hats that fit under helmets, were inferior if sewn out of woven fabric. They had to be knitted, and before the widespread use of knitting machines, women made them one by one.

The labor necessary to outfit an army was enormous, and required organized knitting drives. An autumn 1862 plea for knitters for the Union army in the Civil War quoted a need for four million socks (two pairs per soldier) for the winter. "If the soldiers have to depend entirely on the government," the plea read, "many will have to go without socks, or with poor cotton trash."

The famous World War I effort coordinated by the Red Cross did not start as a patriotic duty. Well before the U.S. got into the war, it was an American volunteer effort to help the wounded and refugees.

"Make a Christmas gift to a wounded, sick, scantily clad, or starving fellow-being through the Red Cross Self-Denial Box!" ran an announcement in 1914. "Presents of yarn and long knitting needles would be very welcome, as all the refugees beg for wool."

By the time the U.S. got into the war in 1917, the Red Cross Production Corps was in high gear, recruiting knitters and regulating yarns and patterns. With the country's own men fighting, the theme changed from humanitarian aid to patriotic duty.

"OUR BOYS NEED SOX—KNIT YOUR BIT," declared a poster from 1917. Clubs competed to produce regiments of sweaters and socks. So many women responded so

KNIT A BIT
FOR OUR FIRST LINE OF DEFENSE
WOOL, NEEDLES AND DIRECTIONS
Comforts Committee of the Navy League
OF THE UNITED STATES
509 FIFTH AVENUE, NEW YORK CITY

enthusiastically—there were more than 6,000 Red Cross knitters in Seattle alone—the military soon put restrictions in place. One rule stated that care packages would not be transported by the military unless the items had been requested by a specific soldier.

That policy was a little clue that hand-knitting for soldiers was abundant, but not always perfect in relevance and fit. In a Mutt and Jeff cartoon of the time, the boys are at sea and receive knitted care packages. While Mutt snuggles into his scarf, Jeff writes a thank-you note reading:

Dear Amy,
Your pair of socks made a hit;
I'm using one for a vest, the other for a mitt.
Who in the Sam Hill taught you to knit?

The harshest critique came from the machine-knitting industry, which was competing with hand-knitters for limited wool supplies. "For God's sake, wake up and stop this hand-knitting," cried Samuel Dale, an expert in machine knitting. He wondered why any wool was available to hand-knitters, when one machine, he said, could do the work of thousands of hand-knitters and keep it up for ten hours a day.

Hand-knitters didn't much dispute the efficiency of knitting machines. But they thought hand-knitting still made a difference. Some soldiers, aviators in particular, were making earnest requests for their work. Then there was the incalculable value of the warmth and heart in a hand-knit item. Some soldiers wrote poems about it and sent them to *Stars and Stripes*. "A.C.G." wrote this about his socks in "To Peggy."

> *Squatting in gleaming camp fire rings*
> *In sunshine and in wet*
> *I'll wear these oozy knitted things*
> *And never will forget*
> *That all that floss was gently rolled*
> *From skein to rolling sphere*
> *By dainty hands I loved to hold*
> *Far far away from here.*

It took only a few appreciative men to motivate a whole nation of knitters all over again, and the machine-knitting protest became nothing but a hiccup. The Red Cross continued to get wool, and knitters went on supplying the troops—for the rest of World War I, and for nearly every war since.

World War II saw another giant Red Cross effort, and Eleanor Roosevelt made a point of knitting in public. Organized hand-knitting supplied the Korean conflict, but seems to have been absent from Vietnam. By the U.S. interventions in Iraq and Afghanistan, it had started again, under grassroots organizations with names like Operation Homefront and Sniper Cozies. Then in 2006, a knitter in Portland, Oregon, Seann McKeel, began dreaming up a new kind of wartime knitalong: a knitalong for peace.

Seann had lived in Japan, and recalled her own visit to the "ground zero" site of the Hiroshima atomic bombing. There she learned the story of Sadako Sasaki, a girl who died of leukemia as an aftereffect of the 1945 explosion. Sadako was active and athletic until she fell sick at the age of eleven. Following a Japanese legend—in which anyone who could fold 1,000 paper cranes would be granted a wish—Sadako hoped to get well. She completed more than 1,000 cranes before dying at the age of twelve.

The strength of her hope and perseverance has inspired countless people the world over to fold 1,000 paper cranes each in an effort to bring peace into their lives and to the earth. Many send their cranes to Hiroshima, where Seann saw strands upon strands of these simple handmade prayers fluttering and glistening in the sun.

These memories inspired Seann to create KnitNot-War 1,0o0, an Internet-driven knitalong in which more than 100 participants are creating 1,000 cranes—out of knitted and felted yarn instead of paper. Her first test knitters were "drunks" at a local bar's weekly craft night, but now knitters from all over the globe are pledging to make ten cranes each, and the work that arrives in her mailbox is affecting.

"The array of cranes is amazing," Seann says. "From super-pristine, tightly folded cranes to these great floppy kid-made ones with glue-gunned sequins." She recalls the first crane that arrived with a child's handwriting on the envelope as an especially moving moment.

The project's goal is no less than peace. When asked if she believes the knitalong will succeed, Seann says without hesitation, "I think it already has."

But she is realistic. She doesn't imagine a magical *poof!* of peace when the final crane is attached to the strand of 1,000. She explains the project has already increased individual knitters' thoughtfulness and has led them to consider issues they may not have otherwise. She's heard from participants who have experienced new peace in their own lives from the act of knitting and felting—very much like the repetitive, tactile act of paper folding.

"It's meditative, but also connects you," Seann says. One crafter e-mailed Seann to say that she finally pinned her grandmother down and got her to teach her the knit and purl stitches, passing on a skill between generations. Other connections are more surprising, such as a call from a "knit for the troops" organizer who wanted to hook up her knitters with Seann's to cross-pollinate both knitalongs.

At first glance, Seann's knitalong for peace and a knitalong for soldiers might seem as opposed as those rival knitalongs in Berlin and Paris during World War I. But that is to assume a lot of things that might be wrong—for example, that knitters supporting the troops support the war. Knitters on opposite sides of any conflict have, above all, common interest in their craft and the gentle comfort it can provide. Those women in Berlin and Paris probably would have had a lot to talk about, if war hadn't gotten in the way.

Knit Your Bit Resources

www.redcross.org/museum/exhibits/knits.asp
American Red Cross museum,
with online exhibition and patterns from
knitting efforts in World Wars I and II.

www.knitnotwar.com
KnitNotWar 1,0o0 project.

www.memory.loc.gov/ammem/sgphtml/sashtml/
The Stars and Stripes from World War I,
available online through the Library of Congress.

Felted Peace Crane

According to Japanese legend, folding 1,000 paper cranes may make a wish come true. Just one of these little knitted and felted birds is delightful as a small gift, ten make a lovely and meaningful garland, and a thousand just might change a life, or the world. DESIGN BY SEANN MCKEEL

FINISHED MEASUREMENTS 12" long, before felting; 9" after felting; 5" after sewing

YARN Brown Sheep Lamb's Pride Worsted (85% wool / 15% mohair; 190 yards / 4 ounces): 1 skein. Shown in #M81 Red Baron and #M11 White Frost. *Note: One skein yields approximately 8 cranes.*

NEEDLES One pair straight needles size US 10½ (6.5 mm)

NOTIONS Tapestry needle

GAUGE Not essential for this project.

NOTES
To make Crane, start with the head, work through neck, cast on to expand body and wings, and decrease down to a tail. Felt this piece of fabric and sew into "folded" bird shape.

2x2 Rib
(multiple of 4 sts + 2; 1-row repeat)
Row 1 (RS): P2, *k2, p2; repeat from * to end.
Row 2: Knit the knit sts and purl the purl sts as they face you.
Repeat Row 2 for 2x2 Rib.

CRANE
Note: Use Backward Loop CO (see page 156) when instructed to CO.

Head
CO 2 sts. Begin St st, beginning with a purl row, CO 1 st at end of each row for next 4 rows, working CO sts in St st–6 sts. Purl 1 row.

Neck
Next Row (RS): Change to 2x2 Rib. Work even for 18 rows.

Body/Wings
Row 1 (RS): P2, k2, p2, CO 5 sts–11 sts.
Row 2: P1, k10, CO 5 sts–16 sts.
Row 3: K1, p14, k1.
SHAPE WINGS
Row 4: CO 2 sts, knit the 2 CO sts, knit the knit sts and purl the purl sts to end–18 sts.
Row 5: CO 2 sts, purl the 2 CO sts, knit the knit sts and purl the purl sts to end–20 sts.
Rows 6-11: Repeat Rows 4 and 5–32 sts.
Row 7: BO 2 sts, work to end–30 sts remain.
Rows 8-12: Repeat Row 7–20 sts remain after Row 12.
Row 13: BO 7 sts, work to end–13 sts remain.
Row 14: Repeat Row 13–6 sts remain.

Tail
Next Row (RS): Change to 2x2 Rib, beginning with k2. Work even for 10 rows.
Shape Tail (RS): Decrease 1 st at beginning of each row for next 5 rows–1 st remains. Fasten off.

FINISHING
Weave in all ends. Place Crane in lingerie bag, set washing machine on hot wash/cold rinse. Add small amount of laundry detergent and pair of jeans or towel for friction. Wash until felted firmly. Or felt by running hot and cold water on Crane, using a little soap and agitating fabric by hand. After felting, shape Crane by creasing neck, head, tail, and wings (see photo). Using tapestry needle, tack wings together at center; tack tail to back of wings so tail stands up; tack back of neck to front of wings so neck stands up; tack head to front of neck to give Crane a beak. Allow to air dry.

Chapter Three
Finding Your Voice

Knitalongs might be about everyone working on the same project, but they don't mean uniformity. In fact, far and away the most entertaining thing about knitalongs is the way they make it so easy to see the influence of the individual knitter on the finished object—an influence above and beyond the pattern.

Seeing a dozen different takes on a great pattern is like hearing ten different musicians play your favorite song—they've each got their own style. Taking in that variety can be a great tool in helping you find and define your own style—your knitting voice.

This chapter looks at three ways knitters can and do find their own creative voices with the help of the knitalong culture. Online knitalongs, coordinated by Internet discussion groups, mailing lists, blogs, and other modes of communication, play a special role. They collect participants from around the world to work on the same project during the same time period and report on their results—almost always with pictures. It's a forum that shows the fantastic variety possible within the execution of a single pattern.

That variety was the whole point of our own Meathead Hat knitalong and online gallery—dozens of people executing the same pattern, each providing their own choices for color and embellishment. The results were an explosion of creativity. The Mothwing Shawl, with its opportunity to blend three colorways of Blue Moon Fiber Arts yarn, is similarly ripe for exploration.

Many knitters also participate in the vibrant world of knitting blogs—online diaries that suck you into a circle of crafters who, in their way, could become as important and intimate to you as your flesh-and-blood friends. Reading and writing blog entries, not to mention taking photographs for them, will help you figure out your own aesthetic. We celebrate the connection between knitting and the written word

with The Pillow of Sei Shonagon—our homage to an ancient Japanese courtier who might just be the world's first blogger—and our Vélo Cycling Sweater, a bike sweater ready to be knitted with your own slogan.

Finally, knitters can express themselves by contributing to a work of art that is larger than themselves. We look at a few knitalongs that are not about making practical items like socks or dishcloths, but are about making people think and feel. And we encourage you to make something wonderfully useless and abstract of your own: a Felted Nest or two.

Online Knitalongs

Three hundred pairs of zigzaggy socks inched their way to life, dangling from about 1,200 double-pointed needles the world over. Knitters from the Netherlands, New Zealand, and New England were all working on the same sock pattern at the same time. It was January 2006, and the Jaywalker Sock knitalong—or "KAL" in online lingo—was making its mark on the Internet.

"It took on a life of its own," says the knitalong host, Cara Davis, a knitter, spinner, writer, and photographer living the fibery life in New Jersey.

Cara found the Jaywalker Sock pattern on the free online knitting magazine *Magknits*. She knitted her first pair and fell in love. From her own website, Cara invited people, no matter where they were, to knit this sock pattern along with her, signing up and relating their experiences in comments on her site.

The response was a mass yarn happening. On Cara's site, the list of participants took up more and more room on the screen, growing to more than 300 names. Some of those people wrote about the knitalong on their own websites too, and like ripples in a pond, it grew larger and reached farther. The Jaywalker pattern designer, Grumperina, got involved by hosting a gallery for pictures of finished socks on her site. That gallery burgeoned into a psychedelic sock-in with more than 500 pairs visible—from the tan and pepper ripples of a sandy-beach-themed pair to the eye-popping curves of a Kool-Aid-dyed set.

"It wasn't the first time this has happened in the knitting world, and I'm sure it won't be the last," says Cara.

Like many organized knit gatherings, online KALs are planned around a central theme or project. Usually it's a pattern, such as the Jaywalker, but it could be a yarn, a designer, even a color. Punny names are common. To name just a few, Zimmermania! is a mutual-support knitalong for Elizabeth Zimmermann fans, Norovember is a knitalong for working with yarns by Noro in the month of November, and Socktober is exactly what it sounds like: a club for knitting socks in October.

Like in-person knitalongs, online KALs come together in many different settings. But instead of cafés, local yarn shops, and living rooms, they're hosted in virtual spaces like bulletin boards, chat rooms, forums, individual or group-written blogs (see "Knitting Blogs" on page 75), and group e-mail lists. Some KALs are focused primarily on sharing photos and are hosted on photo-sharing websites, while others invite participants to write journal entries along with their progress pictures.

Online KALs have been growing in number and accessibility, reports a Cincinnati knitter and mom named Natalie, who has maintained the definitive online list of knitalongs since 2005. Natalie has seen the knitalong concept evolve from small projects, each one started by a core group of blog friends, to far more public events open to anyone in the world, created by one person who feels confident that if she builds a KAL, other knitters will come.

"For the past two years, I've noticed that people start the knitalongs before they have any other participants gathered," she says. "It's also obvious that more of today's KALs are started when the new issues of knitting magazines come out."

Having corralled the knitalongs for a while, Natalie is amazed at how many online KALs are happening—hundreds at a time—and how quickly they get around. She credits the speed and diversity of the Internet as reasons why there is so much virtual joining. And while a knitter who does not participate in online KALs might think the concept sounds cold, the community has a warm glow all its own. Most KAL organizers claim the community is what makes them do it.

"I need to talk to people about my knitting," says Cara. "Not necessarily knit with people around me on the couch, but discuss the yarn and the patterns and the problems. As much as I love my husband, he just can't help when I'm trying to decide which increase to use, you know?"

Online KALs let Cara find advice and camaraderie in abundance, in a way that just wasn't possible before the Internet era. You can see more variety than you could ever see in person—like 140 pointy Meathead Hats, 259 of Elizabeth Zimmermann's Baby Surprise jackets, 60 Ripple Blankets, or 1,200 of Kate Gilbert's Clapotis shawls, each in different waves of color, draped on Adirondack chairs and delicate shoulders from Iceland to Texas, Canada to Japan, Hawaii to Australia.

There is no better way to see a large amount of knitters' work in one place—a whole grassroots gallery of creativity—than an online knitalong. No other gathering place can offer the world in one setting. It's a twenty-four-hour-a-day show-and-tell forum for knitters, and it's growing and changing every minute.

With all that activity, it's easy to meet knitters grappling with the same projects you are, get feedback on color choices, or search for pattern changes and errata. You might even converse with a knitting designer about why she made the choices she did, since designers from the famous to the not-so-known are now dropping in on knitalongs for their own patterns.

Online KALs also have a gritty side, which is one of their defining features. The self-published world of the Internet allows for a raw quality not seen in magazines and books. The ridiculous is not culled from the sublime. Knitters can gain insight by seeing each other's "duds" as well as perfect finished objects. In 2004 knitter and blogger Alison Hansel hosted her first "rip-along" made up entirely of knitters who had duds in progress that needed to be ripped out so the yarn could be reclaimed for more successful projects. She had forty joiners the first year,

411s About Online KALs

knitalongs.xaviermusketeer.com: a frequently updated listing of knitalongs.

knittyboard.com: a highly popular discussion forum associated with the online magazine *Knitty.com*.

januaryone.com: Cara Davis's website.

grumperina.com: the Jaywalker Sock designer's site, with Jaywalker gallery.

knitalong.net: a website from the authors of this book.

and seventy-three when she updated the concept with a February Fix-a-Thon in 2005.

At times, the community is so limitless and vigorous, it gets overwhelming. As Cara, the Jaywalker hostess, notes, "You know your knitalong has really arrived when you start to get backlash," with knitters blogging about how they won't knit the pattern because the KAL is so popular.

For Cara, the greatest surprise of her KAL-hosting career thus far has been how many people participated in the Jaywalker knitalong from around the world. She met the nicest people from—it seemed like—everywhere, and she shared her craft with them without leaving her favorite knitting chair. "It's amazing to think how far and wide your reach can extend through a box on your desk," she says.

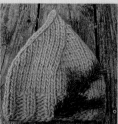

larissa's

MEATHEAD HAT

Knitalong Diary

I hosted my first knitalong in 2004, and I had no idea what I was getting into. I wanted to create an art gallery installation that involved 100 identical knitted hats, each adorned with a numbered cattle ear tag. My idea was an artwork about conformity. The numbered hats would hang in a perfect grid on an impersonal white wall.

As I roasted in the heat of late summer with dozens of pounds of wool on my studio floor, I pondered how I would complete all of the knitting in time for the art opening in October, and I realized I would need a lot of help. I put a note on my blog, asking if anyone would volunteer to knit a hat. Soon I had recruited more than 100 volunteers—the first shock along the way, since I'd expected only a few people would help. I started sending out packages of bulky yarn along with a pattern for what I called a "meathead" hat (I tucked in a tea bag with each kit, as a tiny thank-you).

I was nervous that the hundred or so women who signed up to knit might have a bad experience. They might not have fun or might not feel appreciated enough. I felt unworthy of the help, and more than a little nervous about how I would properly thank everyone.

But what happened was baffling. The volunteers felt that I had given *them* an opportunity. *They* were thanking *me*. Envelope after envelope arrived with meathead hats inside, along with gifts. Gifts! Candy, tea, soaps, even a knitted washcloth that matched my bathroom. The generosity of the volunteers was immense and unexpected.

But the biggest surprises were the hats themselves. Even though they were all made from the same materials and pattern, each one virtually leaped out of its envelope with an individual personality. As I attached the ear tags and hung the hats on the gallery wall, the differences were striking. The meatheads varied in shape, form, size, tightness, twistiness, and character. Some were frighteningly long and strange, others tiny little balls of anxious knitting. A few were

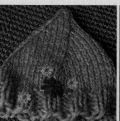

so freakishly shaped they became the sweet under-dogs of the grid.

An art installation that was supposed to be about conforming and giving in to the world's pressures actually became about individuality, the irrepressible personal spirit, and the power of each knitter's hand in her work.

For this book, Martin and I decided to run a new meathead knitalong that didn't just observe that phenomenon, but aided and abetted it. I rewrote the pattern to make the hat a more wearable garment. The pattern encouraged each knitter to make an individual mark by choosing his or her own yarn color and replacing the cattle tag with a fantastic and personal embellishment.

As usual, I ran the knitalong via a website—in this case, my personal blog—and an online picture-sharing site called Flickr.com. I posted an announcement asking for knitalongers. Signup was simple: All someone had to do was send me an e-mail or leave a comment on my blog. Once someone signed up, I e-mailed the pattern out. When knitters finished their hats, they posted

pictures to the online photo-sharing site for everyone to see. There was a deadline and a promise of "door prizes" for a few randomly drawn participants to motivate people to enter and finish.

The result was an explosion of color and whimsy. Mama Urchin set green leaves and red berries of holly on a snow-white cap. Carrie Workman hoisted a pirate flag over a sea of pea green. Gail Fraleigh splayed an ostrich plume on a deep bed of brown. A felted mouse curled up on the brim of a Swiss-cheese-colored hat. A felted snake slithered down the side of another. My favorite was dusky pink and pierced with a giant vintage safety pin, embossed mysteriously with the number 555.

I could go on and on, but the pictures speak so well for themselves. I like to gaze at them all on our website, Knitalong.net, and I hope you will, too.

1. Valerie Wallis, Logan, UT **2.** Carrie Griffin, Portland, OR **3.** Valerie Wallis, Logan, UT **4.** Kathy Hossner, Hillsboro, OR **5.** Carrie Workman, Auburn, WA **6.** Chawne Kimber, Easton, PA **7.** LaDonna, Sausalito, CA **8.** Valerie Wallis, Logan, UT **9.** Jennifer Raab, South Riding, VA **10.** Kathleen Campbell, Huntingtown, MD

Meathead Hat

This hat provides just the foundation for a one-of-a-kind embellishment of your choice—be it an intarsia pirate patch, a giant safety pin, a plastic flower, or a crayon holster. The stitches are basic, but they are made with two strands of a slightly shiny yarn that adds just a hint of light and complexity.

SIZES Child (Adult Small/Medium, Large)

FINISHED MEASUREMENTS 17 (18^3/$_4$, 20^1/$_2$)" circumference. *Note: Hat stretches easily.*

YARN Brown Sheep Lamb's Pride Bulky (85% wool / 15% mohair; 125 yards / 4 ounces): 1 (2, 2) skeins. Shown in #M162 Mulberry (Child) and #M175 Bronze Patina (Large). Crayon holster designed by Heidi Butler (optional).

NEEDLES One pair of straight needles size US 15 (10 mm); one pair of straight needles size US 10 (6 mm) (optional, for Crayon Holster). Change needle size if necessary to obtain correct gauge.

NOTIONS One optional embellishment, such as vintage button, big plastic flower, or 3 crayons

GAUGE 9 sts and 13 rows = 4" (10 cm) in Stockinette stitch (St st) using larger needles and 2 strands of yarn held together

2x2 Rib
(multiple of 4 sts + 2; 1-row repeat)
Row 1 (RS): K2, *p2, k2; rep from * to end.
Row 2: Knit the knit sts and purl the purl sts as they face you.
Repeat Row 2 for 2x2 Rib.

HAT
With 2 strands of yarn held together and using larger needles, CO 38 (42, 46) sts. Begin 2x2 Rib. Work even for 6 rows, ending with a WS row.
Next Row (RS): Change to St st; work even for 6 (8, 8) rows.

SHAPE HAT
SIZE LARGE ONLY
Setup Row (RS): K1, *k9, k2tog; rep from * to last st, k1–42 sts rem. Purl 1 row.

SIZES SMALL/MEDIUM AND LARGE
Next Row (RS): K1, *k8, k2tog; rep from * to last st, k1–38 sts rem. Purl 1 row.

ALL SIZES
Row 1: K1, *k7, k2tog; rep from * to last st, k1–34 sts rem.
Row 2 (and all WS Rows): Purl.
Row 3: K1, *k6, k2tog; rep from * to last st, k1–30 sts rem.
Row 5: K1, *k5, k2tog; rep from * to last st, k1–26 sts rem.
Row 7: K1, *k4, k2tog; rep from * to last st, k1–22 sts rem.
Row 9: K1, *k3, k2tog; rep from * to last st, k1–18 sts rem.
Row 11: K1, *k2, k2tog; rep from * to last st, k1–14 sts rem.
Row 13: K1, *k1, k2tog; rep from * to last st, k1–10 sts rem.
Row 15 and 17: K1, *k2tog; rep from * to last st, k1–4 sts rem after Row 17.
Row 19: *K2tog; rep from * to end–2 sts rem. Pass first st over last st and off the needle–1 st rem. Cut yarn, leaving a 6" tail. Draw through rem st, pull tight and fasten off.

FINISHING
Sew back seam. Weave in ends. Sew on embellishment.

CRAYON HOLSTER (OPTIONAL)
Using 1 strand of yarn and smaller needles, CO 10 sts and work in St st for 10 rows, beginning with a knit row. Change to 1x1 Rib. Work even for 4 rows. BO all sts in pattern. Sew CO edge and side edges of Holster to Hat; fill with crayons.

Mothwing Shawl

Moths and knitters don't usually mix, but perhaps this shawl—with its graduated color changes and winglike effect—will offer a place to meet peacefully. A knitter's delight, the shawl is made of three colorways of Blue Moon Fiber Arts's® amazing Socks that Rock® yarn which blend into one another throughout a series of mitered triangles and one giant diamond.

FINISHED MEASUREMENTS 61" wide at widest point x 26" long at back center

YARN Blue Moon Fiber Arts® Socks that Rock® heavyweight (100% superwash merino; 350 yards / 7 ounces): 1 hank each Obsidian (A), Henpecked (B), and Rooster Rock (C); Debbie Bliss Baby Cashmerino (55% merino wool / 33% microfiber / 12% cashmere; 137 yards / 50 grams): 1 hank #011 Chocolate (D)

NEEDLES One 24" (61 cm) long circular (circ) needle size US 7 (4.5 mm). Change needle size if necessary to obtain correct gauge.

NOTIONS Crochet hook size US F/5 (4.0 mm)

GAUGE 20 sts and 26 rows = 4" (10 cm) in Stockinette stitch (St st) with A

SHAWL

Triangle (make 2)

Note: Work decreases at beginning and end of row loosely.
With A, CO 183 sts. Knit one row.

Shape Triangle

Row 1 (RS): Ssk, k87, [ssk] twice, k2tog, knit to last 2 sts, k2tog–178 sts rem.
Row 2 and all WS Rows: Purl.
Row 3: Ssk, knit to 2 sts before first ssk of last RS row, ssk, [k2tog] twice, knit to last 2 sts, k2tog–173 sts rem.
Row 5: Ssk, knit to 1 st before first ssk of last RS row, [ssk] twice, k2tog, knit to last 2 sts, k2tog–168 sts rem.

Rows 7-22: Rep Rows 3-6–128 sts rem after Row 21.
Row 23: Change to B; do not cut A. Rep Row 3–123 sts rem.
Row 25: Change to A; do not cut B. Rep Row 5–118 sts rem.
Rows 27-30: Rep Rows 23-26–108 sts rem after Row 29.
Row 31: Change to B; cut A, leaving a 6" tail. Rep Row 3–103 sts rem.
Row 33: Rep Row 5–98 sts rem.
Rows 35-46: Rep Rows 3-6–68 sts rem after Row 46.
Row 47: Change to C; do not cut B. Rep Row 3–63 sts rem.
Row 49: Change to B; do not cut C. Rep Row 5–58 sts rem.
Rows 51-54: Rep Rows 47-50–48 sts rem after Row 53.
Row 55: Change to C; cut B, leaving a 6" tail. Rep Row 3–43 sts rem.
Row 57: Rep Row 5–38 sts rem.
Rows 59-70: Rep Rows 3-6–8 sts rem after Row 69.
Row 71: [Ssk] twice, [k2tog] twice–4 sts rem. BO all sts purlwise.

Diamond

With WS of first Triangle facing (you will have a purl bump on RS), beginning at center of CO edge (see Schematic, point A) and working toward long side of triangle, with A, pick up and knit 90 sts along side of Triangle, ending 1 st before corner (point B); with WS of second Triangle facing, pick up and knit 1 st from last st of first Triangle together with first st of second Triangle (you will join the two Triangles together with this picked-up st), pick up and knit 90 sts along side of second Triangle to center of CO edge (point C)–181 sts.

SHAPE DIAMOND

Note: Slip all sts knitwise.
Row 1 (RS): Slip 1, k87, [ssk] twice, k2tog, knit to end–178 sts rem.

Row 2 (and all WS Rows): Slip 1, purl to end.

Row 3: Slip 1, knit to 2 sts before first ssk of last RS row, ssk, [k2tog] twice, knit to end–175 sts rem.

Row 5: Slip 1, knit to 1 st before first ssk of last RS row, [ssk] twice, k2tog, knit to end–172 sts rem.

Rows 7-22: Rep Rows 3-6–148 sts rem after Row 21.

Row 23: Change to B; do not cut A. Rep Row 3–145 sts rem.

Row 25: Change to A; do not cut B. Rep Row 5–142 sts rem.

Rows 27-30: Rep Rows 23-26–136 sts rem after Row 29.

Row 31: Change to B; cut A, leaving a 6" tail. Rep Row 3–133 sts rem.

Row 33: Rep Row 5–130 sts rem.

Rows 35-46: Rep Rows 3-6–112 sts rem after Row 45.

Row 47: Change to C; do not cut B. Rep Row 3–109 sts rem

Row 49: Change to B; do not cut C. Rep Row 5–106 sts rem.

Rows 51-54: Rep Rows 47-50–100 sts rem after Row 53.

Row 55: Change to C; cut B, leaving a 6" tail. Rep Row 3–97 sts rem.

Row 57: Rep Row 5–94 sts rem.

Rows 59-114: Rep Rows 3-6–10 sts rem after Row 113.

Row 115: Rep Row 3–7 sts rem.

Row 117: Slip 1, k1, dcd, k2–5 sts rem.

Row 119: Slip 1, dcd, k1–3 sts rem.

Row 121: Dcd–1 st rem. Fasten off.

FINISHING

Weave in ends. Wet Shawl, block to measurements, and allow to air dry. Crochet Edging: Rnd 1 (RS): With RS facing, using crochet hook and D, beginning 1 st up from one corner of Shawl, work single crochet (sc) in each edge st around Shawl (making sure not to work sts too tightly), working 3 scs in each corner st to turn corner; slip st to join beginning of rnd; turn work. Rnd 2 (WS): Loosely work slip st in each sc around Shawl; slip st to join beginning of rnd. Fasten off. Weave in all ends. Reblock Shawl.

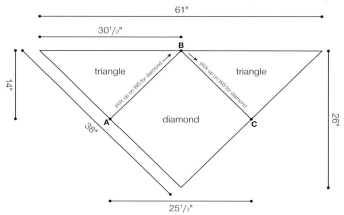

Knitting Blogs

Angela Tong is perhaps the last person you'd call isolated or reserved. "I'm not shy," she declares, with a laugh that cuts through a crowd. Angela lives in a Brooklyn brownstone with 8 million New Yorkers around her, kids yelling in the street outside, and a thundering subway under the pavement. A custom jeweler, Angela shares a studio with a fashion designer and a home with a husband and two frantic, lovable miniature dogs. On a recent birthday Angela was taken by friends and family to not one, nor two, but three impenetrably popular restaurants.

Still, there's a part of her that's lonely. She doesn't have any *crafty* friends in town. The one she had moved upstate years ago, and her other friends, as close as they are, make jokes about her "grandma hobbies." She'd be lost without that gray box upstairs—her computer—and her connection to the world of Internet knitters.

Every morning she makes a huge mug of tea, scoops up the dogs, and fires up that box to take a little tour through the lives of her craft buddies. She's never met them in person, but she knows a lot about them anyway: their cats' names, their kids' toothaches, and most especially what they are knitting. Sometimes she just reads and moves on, other times she leaves a comment.

"Oh! He is so cute!" she writes about one pal's Japanese-style stuffed-toy creation. "Happy b-day to your brother!" she pipes in about another's new family snapshots. And about a new afghan, one simple word: "Gorgeous."

Then, when she's got something of her own to announce—say, a clever baby blanket made out of a giant afghan square, or a sweet batch of chocolate hazelnut cookies—she logs on to her own website, writes something up, and pastes in photos. Within a day or two, friends have come 'round.

"Those cookies look divine," writes a Brit named schrodinger.

"Nice colors for a baby blanket!" writes Amy from the American Midwest. "The right color choices can elevate the simple pastel to something more sophisticated."

Angela's computer is her lifeline to the world of weblogs, or blogs. It's social networking for the 21st century. Where Victorians had letters of introduction and calling cards, knitters now have blogs and comments.

Though every Internet technology helps knitters communicate, nothing seems as ideal for the craft as the blog. A knitting blog is an online diary and scrapbook where words are easily mixed with pictures. It's a highly personal record available for the whole world to see. Daily or weekly entries are perfect to showcase progress on a knitting project, with each new inch of a sweater being watched by sympathetic friends. The informal format encourages asides and tangents too. Suffering through school plays, odes to sexy actors, bizarre family recipes—quirky subjects give sharp bloggers a chance to express their personalities and draw their readers close.

"I stumbled on blogs by accident," Angela says. "I was astounded! I loved the fact that people shared their lives and their knitting online."

"It was like a whole new world opened up," says Becky, a pediatric nurse from Ohio. "Suddenly I was a fascinated observer of a cyberfamily of knitters."

"I always learn something," says Cheryl, a retired church secretary from Arkansas. "They [other bloggers] are more adventurous than I would be!"

For Angela, blogs provide a gallery of creativity outside the confines of knitting magazines. She's been inspired to create things she never would have otherwise. For example, her giant square baby blanket was a riff on an afghan square she made in a knitalong for this book's Barn-Raising Quilt (page 149).

Like Angela, you might start a blog as a simple record of craft projects, but reading and writing about knitting, taking photographs of finished objects, and knowing there are a few people out there watching can press you to express your own idea of beauty. "It's a real motivation," Angela says.

As you enter the community of blog readers and writers, you'll gravitate to those you respect. You may find yourself making friends with someone who lives 9,000 miles away, and supporting each other in more than your knitting lives.

Rachael Herron of Oakland, California, received so much companionship and inspiration from her knitting blog, Yarn-A-Go-Go, that she started a knitters-who-run blog too, where each of several hundred fitness-oriented knitters can read and post diary entries.

"I click, and LO AND BEHOLD," Rachael writes, "someone else has blogged, and they tell me what they're doing, and in doing so, they encourage me to keep going. Little miracles, every time I turn the computer on."

Blogs make a whole world of knitterly companionship and expertise available twenty-four hours a day. It's a blessing and an addiction. Since most blogs contain a list—or "blogroll"—of links to other blogs, it's easy to get lost for hours. It's an overwhelmingly *female* world. As most knitters are females, so are most knit bloggers—currently more than 95 percent. It's an overwhelmingly supportive world. If you ask a thoughtful question, someone will almost always respond.

And it's an overwhelmingly positive world. Many blogs are clean, neat spaces that make life and knitting look just a little too perfect—but invitingly so. Though a frustrated rant, whether it's about a popular pattern or a slow-witted kitchen remodeler, can be one of the most entertaining and endearing types of blog entries, abundant negativity is looked down upon. Comments that are mean and personal in nature, or criticism that is not constructive, may get booed out of town by a blog's loyal regular readers. And though craft blogs come in a multitude of flavors, most don't mix heavy subjects, such as strident

{ *getting going in the blogosphere* }

www.technorati.com: useful for finding blogs that are sometimes left out of standard Internet searches.

www.bloglines.com, www.kinja.com, and www.reader.google.com: all provide software that helps you read your favorite blogs from one centralized site— a time-saver for the true addict!

When you're ready to launch your own blog, several sites—www.typepad.com, www.wordpress.com, and www.blogger.com among them—all provide easy-to-use software, with free and paid options.

Photo-sharing sites, such as www.flickr.com, provide a place for storing and organizing your photos before you select those that will go into your blog entries, and sites such as www.bighugelabs.com offer fun "toys" to create photo mosaics and more.

politics, with knitting. It's as if the knitting relationships are too tender, and too precious, to mix with tragedy and politics, no matter how real and common those things are.

"If there's too much of that stuff, it can be a downer," says Angela. She likes the blogs she reads, and the one she writes, to stay on the positive side of things. "It's the place I escape to," she admits with a laugh. "It's my happy place."

The Pillow of Sei Shonagon

Sei Shonagon, a courtier to an ancient Japanese empress, just might be the original blogger. A connoisseur of beauty and words both, she started a diary of her own thoughts, which was promptly discovered by her peers and celebrated as gossipy entertainment. Her Pillow Book, completed around AD 1000, is a collection of poems, lists, and diarizing so eloquent and nervy that she seems more contemporary and alive than most of the people writing today. This pattern is an homage to her obsessive sensitivities in subjects as diverse as colors, textures, handwriting, and the proper way to wake a lover. The face of the pillow is knitted lace in linen, woven through with a ribbon carrying a special message—in this case, Shonagon's list of "things that make one's heart beat faster."

FINISHED MEASUREMENTS Approximately 17" wide x 12" high

YARN Lovet Sales Euroflax Originals Linen Sport Weight (100% linen; 270 yards / 100 grams): 1 hank #70 White

NEEDLES One pair straight needles size US 3 (3.25 mm). Change needle size if necessary to obtain correct gauge.

NOTIONS $1/2$ yard 45" wide cotton muslin fabric in white, or any coordinating light color; enough thin fusible interfacing to back entire piece of muslin; sewing needle; matching thread; 12" x 16" pillow form; steam iron; yardstick or quilting template; quilt tracing wheel or very light pencil and eraser; permanent fabric marker; scissors; blocking pins; safety pins; preferred text

GAUGE 22 sts and 32 rows = 4" (10 cm) in Eyelet Pattern

Eyelet Pattern

(multiple of 2 sts; 4-row repeat)
Row 1 (WS): Purl.
Rows 2 and 3: Purl.
Row 4: *Yo, skp; repeat from * to end.
Repeat Rows 1-4 for Eyelet Pattern.

PILLOW

Top

CO 94 sts. Work Garter st (knit every row) for 10 rows.
Next Row (WS): K6 (border; keep in Garter st), work in Eyelet Pattern to last 6 sts, k6 (border; keep in Garter st). Work even for 83 rows, ending on Row 3 of Eyelet Pattern.
Next Row (RS): Change to Garter st. Work even for 10 rows. BO all sts loosely.

Text Strips

Cut muslin into 2 rectangles, $18^1/2$" x $12^1/2$" each. Cut interfacing into 2 rectangles, 18" x 12" each. Back both pieces of muslin with interfacing, using a hot, steamy iron, leaving a $1/2$" border around interfacing. Set aside 1 rectangle for Bottom. Use the other rectangle to write text. Using yardstick or quilting template as a guide, mark straight lines across second rectangle every $1/2$", with tracing wheel or very light pencil. You should end up with twenty-five $1/2$" wide rows. Do not cut rows.

Using fabric marker, write your chosen text. *Note: You will need only 20 strips for the finished pillow, so you have 5 rows for mistakes or practice.* Allow text to dry completely. Cut along traced lines so you have 20 strips of text. Erase any pencil marks if necessary.

FINISHING

Block Top to 18" x 12½". Weave Text Strips through eyelets. If you wish, skip some holes so the weaving is more random and larger bits of text show (see photos). Begin and end each row with the Text Strips tucked under the knitted border. Safety pin around entire edge of Top to secure Text Strips.

With WS's together, pin second muslin rectangle (Bottom) to Top. Hand-sew pieces together around three sides using back stitch, making sure to catch edge of each Text Strip as you sew. Turn RS-out. Insert pillow form and sew up remaining side. Remove all pins. *Note: Edges will fray slightly over time; you can give them a start by fraying them with your fingers.*

TEXT USED

From *The Pillow Book of Sei Shonagon*, Volume 1, translated and edited by Ivan Morris, Copyright 1967 Ivan Morris. Reprinted by permission of Columbia University Press (US and Philippines) and Oxford University Press (rest of world).

Things That Make One's Heart Beat Faster
Sparrows feeding their young. To pass a place where babies are playing. To sleep in a room where some fine incense has been burnt. To notice that one's elegant Chinese mirror has become a little cloudy. To see a gentleman stop his carriage before one's gate and instruct his attendants to announce his arrival. To wash one's hair, make one's toilet, and put on scented robes; even if not a soul sees one, these preparations still produce an inner pleasure. It is night and one is expecting a visitor. Suddenly one is startled by the sound of rain-drops, which the wind blows against the shutters.

Vélo Cycling Sweater

Knitting words into fabric is an ancient practice, but some of our favorite letterwork is only as old as the double-diamond bike frame. Before Lycra and fleece, cyclists in events like the Tour de France sported wool cycling jerseys, usually blazoned with their sponsors' names in the loudest of type. Here we offer a pattern so you can do the same. Create your own slogan (ours says "tough guy" in French, or more literally, "hard to cook"), or draw a personal logo. Alphabet charts are available in many knitting stitch dictionaries and online, or you can use knitter's graph paper to draw your own letters and pictures—even if your sponsor is simply "Mom." DESIGN BY ADRIAN BIZILIA

SIZES

To fit 34-36 (38-40, 42-44, 46-48)" chest
Small (Medium, Large, X-Large)
Shown in size Medium, Men's length

FINISHED MEASUREMENTS

36 (40, 44, 48)" chest
Note: There are two lengths for this sweater, a women's length and a men's length. The first set of figures is for the women's length; the second set of figures, shown between <>, is for the men's length. Where only one set of figures is given, it applies to both lengths.
$25^1/_2$ ($26^1/_2$, 28, 29)", < $28^1/_2$ ($29^1/_2$, 31, 32)" > long

YARN

Araucania Nature Wool (100% wool; 240 yards / 100 grams):
4 (4, 5, 5) < 4 (4, 5, 6) > hanks #19 (MC); 1 (1, 2, 2) hanks #35 (A); 1 hank #52 (B)

NEEDLES

One 16" (40 cm) long circular (circ) needle size US 6 (4 mm)
One 29" (74 cm) long circular needle size US 6 (4 mm)
One set of five double-pointed needles (dpn) size US 6 (4 mm)
One 29" (74 cm) long circular needle size US 4 (3.5 mm)
One set of five double-pointed needles size US 4 (3.5 mm)
Change needle size if necessary to obtain correct gauge.

NOTIONS

Stitch markers; stitch holders; waste yarn in contrasting color; 6 yarn bobbins; sewing needle and thread to match MC; one zipper $9^1/_2$ ($9^1/_2$, 10, $10^1/_2$)" < 10 (10, $10^1/_2$, 11)" > to match MC. *Note: For best results, buy zipper after you've finished sweater and measured opening. Any row gauge change will affect zipper length needed. Alternatively, you may buy a longer zipper and trim bottom to fit.*

GAUGE

20 sts and 27 rows = 4" (10 cm) in Stockinette stitch (St st) using larger needles

NOTES

The body of the Sweater is worked in the round from CO to the beginning of the colorwork, then Front and Back are worked separately to the armholes. The Sleeves are worked in the round from CO to the armhole, where they are joined with the Front and Back for the Yoke. The Sweater is again worked in the round until the neck split, after which it is worked back and forth to the end.

2x2 Rib

(multiple of 4 sts; 1-rnd repeat)
All Rnds: P1, *k2, p2; repeat from * to last 3 sts, k2, p1.

SWEATER

Sleeves (make 2)

With smaller dpns and MC, CO 36 (40, 44, 48) sts. Join for working in the rnd, being careful not to twist sts; place marker (pm) for beginning of rnd. Begin 2x2 Rib. Work even for 8 rnds.

Next Rnd: Change to B; knit 1 rnd. Change to 2x2 Rib. Work even for 3 rnds.

Next Rnd: Change to A; knit 1 rnd. Change to 2x2 Rib. Work even for 3 rnds.

Next Rnd: Change to MC; knit 1 rnd. Change to 2x2 Rib. Work even for 7 rnds.

SHAPE SLEEVE

Note: Change to circ needle when necessary for number of sts on needles.

Setup Rnd: Change to larger dpns. P1, [k2, p2] twice, pm, k1, m1, k16 (20, 24, 28), m1, k1, pm, [p2, k2] twice, p1–38 (42, 46, 50) sts. Work even for 4 rnds, working increased sts in St st.

Increase Rnd: Work to 1 st after first marker, m1, work to 1 st before next marker, m1, work to end–40 (44, 48, 52) sts. Repeat Increase Rnd every 5 rnds 16 times–72 (76, 80, 84) sts. Work even until piece measures 19^1/$_2$ (20, 20^1/$_2$, 21)" < 21^1/$_2$ (22, 22^1/$_2$, 23)" > from the beginning. Cut yarn; transfer first and last 9 sts to holder for underarm; transfer remaining 54 (58, 62, 66) sts to waste yarn for Yoke.

Body

With MC and smaller 29" circ needle, CO 180 (200, 220, 240) sts. Join for working in the rnd, being careful not to twist sts; pm for beginning of rnd. Work as for Sleeve to beginning of Sleeve shaping.

Next Rnd: Change to larger 29" circ needle. P1, [k2, p2] twice, k72 (82, 92, 102), [p2, k2] 4 times, p2, knit to last 9 sts, [p2, k2] twice, p1. Work even until piece measures 6^1/$_2$ (7, 7^1/$_2$, 8)" < 8^1/$_2$ (9, 9^1/$_2$, 10)" > from the beginning. Transfer last 90 (100, 110, 120) sts worked to waste yarn or separate circ needle for Back.

Front

Row 1 (RS): K1, m1-p, [k2, p2] twice, k12 (17, 22, 27), pm, work Chart A across 48 sts, pm, knit to last 9 sts, [p2, k2] twice, m1-p, k1–92 (102, 112, 122) sts.

Row 2: P1, k1, work to last 2 sts, k1, p1. Work even until entire Chart is complete. Cut A.

Next Row (RS): Continuing in MC only, work even for 2 rows. Cut MC.

Next Row (RS): Change to A. Knit.

Next Row (WS): P1, k1, [p2, k2] twice, p72 (82, 92, 102), [k2, p2] twice, k1, p1. Work even for 4 rows.

Next Row (RS): Work to first marker, work Chart B to next marker, work to end. Work even until entire Chart is complete.

Next Row (RS): Continuing in A only, work even for 6 rows, removing markers on last row. Cut A. Transfer sts to waste yarn or separate circ needle for Yoke.

Back

Row 1 (RS): K1, m1-p, [k2, p2] twice, knit to last 9 sts, [p2, k2] twice, m1-p, k1–92 (102, 112, 122) sts.

Row 2: P1, k1, work to last 2 sts, k1, p1. Work even for 16 rows. Cut MC.

Next Row (RS): Change to A. Knit.

Next Row (WS): P1, k1, [p2, k2] twice, purl to last 10 sts, [k2, p2] twice, k1, p1. Work even for 46 rows. Cut A.

Yoke

With MC and same needle, knit across 54 (58, 62, 66) sts from left Sleeve, pm, transfer first 10 sts of Front to st holder for armhole, knit to last 10 sts of Front, pm, transfer next 10 sts to st holder for armhole, knit across 54 (58, 62, 66) sts from right Sleeve, transfer next 10 sts of Back to st holder for armhole, pm, knit to last 10 sts of Back, transfer next 10 sts to st holder for armhole–252 (280, 308, 336) sts. Join for working in the rnd; pm for beginning of rnd. Begin St st. Work even until Yoke measures ^{1}/$_2$" < 1" >.

Begin Neck Slit: Knit to 36 (41, 46, 51) sts after first marker, turn.

Next Row (WS): Purl, turn. Working back and forth, work in St st until Yoke measures 1" < 2" >, ending with a WS row.

SHAPE YOKE

Decrease Row (RS): [Knit to 2 sts before marker, ssk, slip marker (sm), k2tog] 4 times, knit to end–244 (272, 300, 328) sts remain. Repeat Decrease Row every other row 21 (21, 23, 24) times, ending with a WS row–76 (104, 116, 136) sts remain.

Shape Neck (RS): Continuing Yoke shaping as established, BO 5 (6, 9, 10) sts at beginning of next 2 rows, then decrease 1 st each neck edge every other row 3 (5, 5, 6) times–28 (34, 40, 48) sts remain. Cut yarn; set aside.

FINISHING

Collar

With RS facing, using smaller circ needle, join MC to BO sts at right neck edge, pick up and knit 4 (5, 6, 7) sts from BO sts, 7 (9, 10, 13) sts along right Front neck edge, knit across 28 (34, 34, 42) sts from Yoke, pick up and knit 7 (9, 10, 13) sts along left Front neck edge, and 4 (5, 6, 7) sts from BO sts–50 (62, 66, 82) sts.

Rows 1 and 3 (WS): P2, *k2, p2; repeat from * to end.

Rows 2 and 4: Knit the knit sts and purl the purl sts as they face you.

Row 5: Change to B. Purl.

Row 6: K2, *p2, k2; repeat from * to end.

Row 7: Change to A. Purl.

Row 8: Repeat Row 6.

Row 9: Change to MC. Purl.

Row 10: Repeat Row 6.

Row 11: P2, *k2, p2; repeat from * to end.

Row 12: Repeat Row 6. BO all sts loosely in pattern.

Sew side seams, including first st from each armhole st holder, leaving 18 sts on st holders for each armhole. Using Three-Needle BO (page 157), graft live sts of Sleeves and Body at underarms. Weave in ends. Block Sweater.

Zipper

Using waste yarn, baste Neck Slit edges together. Pin zipper into place with zipper teeth centered between Front edges. With RS facing, sew zipper to edge, one st in from edge. Sew firmly across bottom of opening, through zipper. Remove waste yarn. Cut zipper to length, if needed.

CHART A

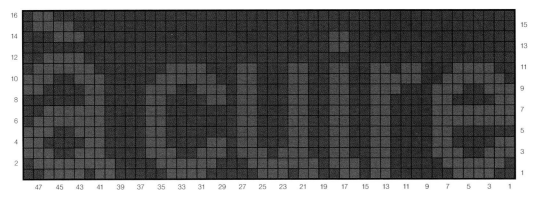

CHART B

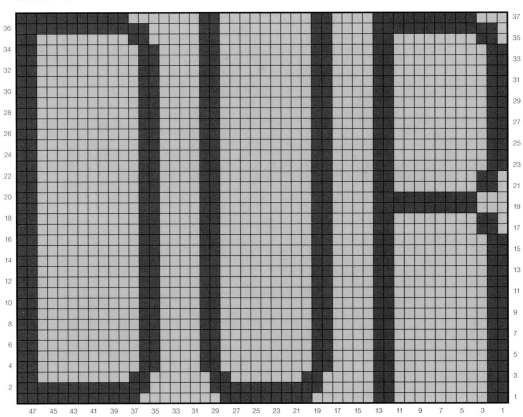

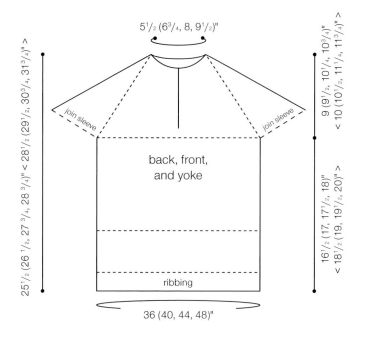

5½ (6¾, 8, 9½)"

9 (9½, 10¼, 10¾)"
< 10 (10½, 11¼, 11¾)" >

25½ (26½, 27¾, 28¾)" < 28½ (29¼, 30¾, 31¾)" >

join sleeve

back, front,
and yoke

join sleeve

16½ (17, 17½, 18)"
< 18½ (19, 19½, 20)" >

ribbing

36 (40, 44, 48)"

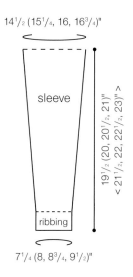

14½ (15¼, 16, 16¾)"

sleeve

19½ (20, 20½, 21)"
< 21½, 22, 22½, 23)" >

ribbing

7¼ (8, 8¾, 9½)"

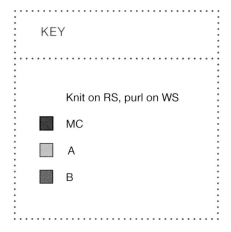

KEY

Knit on RS, purl on WS

■ MC

□ A

■ B

CHART NOTES

You may find it easiest to use a combination of the Intarsia Colorwork Method and the Stranded (Fair-Isle) Colorwork Method (see page 157) to work the Charts.

When working Chart A, use the Stranded Colorwork Method. When working Chart B, use the Intarsia Colorwork Method, using a separate bobbin or strand of yarn for each leg of each letter (6 bobbins total).

Fine Art Knitalongs

The sweaters must be red. They must be acrylic—Red Heart brand, in colors like Flame Red, Jockey Red, and Cherry Red. And they must be tiny—just three inches across the chest. Despite these apparently rigid rules, when lined up in a photo gallery, the little sweaters each glow with individuality. One seems to be waving frantically, loose ends flying from its sleeves. Another, with little yarn balls dangling from each arm, seems to be carrying buckets of water. One sits so self-contained, it seems to stare straight into the viewer's soul. Each one brings to mind a single living, breathing life.

That's just how Nina Rosenberg intended this knitalong art project, the Red Sweater Deployment Project, to work. The knitalong represents individual American lives lost in the war in Iraq. Each sweater corresponds to a single soldier's life. More than that, each sweater is made by the hands of an individual volunteer, giving it its own quirks and qualities. Nina has displayed hundreds of these sweaters linked together on a cord in galleries and draped from a tree outside her house, a poignant witness to distant events.

Nina is adamant the project is not a war protest—it's meant to invoke thoughtfulness.

"I felt a need to make other people more aware of what is going on so far away," Nina writes of her work, "to compel people to listen to the news, ask questions, form opinions, or to simply take a moment to stop and consider the realities of war and how it is affecting their lives, even if they are not directly involved."

The red sweaters illustrate a powerful kind of knitting together—an artistic knitalong in which the interaction among crafters and the personal hand of each knitter are central to the message. For this kind of collaborative artwork, a coordinating artist often provides guidelines and then collects pieces from numerous knitters. The coordinating artist then joins or installs the knitted pieces together. Other times, volunteers actually knit together on a single work. It's a way to make an artistic impression with an impact unlike any single artist's work.

Certain themes seem inseparably linked to knitted artwork. The irregular, homely forms of knitting symbolize domesticity and comfort, so the great majority of knitted artworks play off that connotation, often in the form of knitted coverings, or "cozies," for inanimate objects. Some of the most interesting pieces have an impact that is as poetic as political.

In 2002, the Stump Cozy Project in Astoria, Oregon, engaged dozens of artists—some of them knitters, some not—covering tree stumps at a logging site. Fresh logging sites are a vision of destruction, and the cozies were incongruous and touching tiny comforts in a world of damage. More subtle was a house cozy made in 1999 by Janet Morton, a pioneer of the cozy-art genre, who completely covered a cottage with more than 800 recycled sweaters. Throughout fall and winter, tens of thousands of visitors came by ferry to see the installation, which was shown in a wooded area on Ward's Island in Toronto.

In Denmark, in spring 2006, artist Marianne Jorgensen and a team of hardworking volunteers spent days sewing more than 4,000 pink knitted squares around a World War II era battle tank parked in the street outside a museum. The squares had been knitted by volunteers from around the planet, resulting in a "tank cozy" that positively radiated (see photo on page 88). Other knitted artwork calls attention to something that seems a foil to that warm, homey sense, like war or nationalism. Sabrina Gschwandtner's 2007 *Wartime Knitting Circle* installation in New York welcomed visitors to the Museum of Arts & Design to sit down—amid historical photos of wartime knitalongs—and knit comforts, such as socks, slippers, and helmet liners, for contemporary soldiers. Photos of the installation show a wide diversity of participants knitting, while black-and-white photos of past wartime knitters hover, ghostly, behind them.

In the summer of 2005, artist Dave Cole supervised two immense John Deere excavators as they wielded knitting needles the size of telephone poles, all to knit a giant American flag at the Massachusetts Museum of Contemporary Art.

Often knitted art projects explore volume, and they require a very large number of similar objects or pieces to make an impact. Knitting *along* is especially well suited

installations, such as Seann McKeel's KnitNotWar 1,0o0 project—an installation of 1,000 felted origami-style cranes (see pages 58 and 61).

Knitting along is also especially suited to artworks that explore the repetition inherent in the craft, and variation within structure. Some knitalongs may simply explore the very act of knitting and the repetitive, meditative, sometimes obsessively enjoyable motion of making stitches.

Performance artist Kristina Wong collected unfinished knitting to use as part of the set for her solo performance show *Wong Flew Over the Cuckoo's Nest*. Initially an exploration of the high incidence of mental illness among Asian-American women, her show is billed as "a semi-autobiographical, serio-comic quest for a cheap fix to eradicate depression, anxiety, and all-out neuroses." She used knitters' half-baked creations as a representation of incomplete intentions, women's work, and loneliness. For hundreds of knitters, sending in an old WIP (work in progress) made this the easiest art knitalong they'd ever been part of.

Shane Waltener has explored connectedness quite literally, with live simultaneous knitalongs. One of his performance/installation pieces featured four or five knitters sitting in a tight group with their backs to one another, working simultaneously on long circular needles. They were knitting a single donut-shaped piece of fabric with no beginning or end, and as they worked, the knitted piece rotated around the group. His other works include knitalongs in parks and other public places, with giant cobweb-like lace works as the result.

Other art knitalongs make less literal connections. The *Knitting Map* was a 2005 artwork that spanned space and time and involved a knitalong unlike any before. A satellite far above the earth tracked traffic and weather patterns in Cork, Ireland. Far below that satellite, in the crypt of St. Luke's Church, dozens of knitters sat bent over their work every day for a year, responding to that live data with changes in stitch patterns and yarn colors. Over the year 2005, almost 2,500 volunteer knitters from twenty-two countries, aged from three to eighty-two, contributed to the project, which was commissioned by the city of Cork and created by the arts and performance group half/angel. The work used knitting—"some hefty cabling during rush hour; quiet lulls of stocking stitch on Sunday mornings"—to take the pulse of the city for twelve months.

Clearly, artists gain from the free labor of volunteer knitalongers. And audiences gain immense and sometimes deeply moving works to experience. But what do the knitters get out of this process?

Nina Rosenberg has collected comments from hundreds of people about their motivations for collaborating with her by knitting tiny red sweaters. Some are overtly political, speaking of the toll of war and the enormous scale of it.

"I knit for the future of my grandchildren," writes one anonymous red sweater knitter. "May they grow up in a peaceful, just world where all are counted."

Others want to be part of something bigger than themselves, or to honor a particular soldier. And some want to give something back to the knitting community they feel has enriched them. It may be the first time they've ever considered themselves artists—which is a milestone along the way to finding their own knitting voices.

Exploring Knitted Art

www.redsweaters.org
Home page for the Red Sweater Deployment Project.

www.theknittingmachine.com
Home page for artist Dave Cole.

www.kristinawong.com
Home page for artist Kristina Wong.

www.shanewaltener.com
Home page for artist Shane Waltener.

www.knitknit.net/sabrina/inst_wartime_01.html
Web page featuring Sabrina Gschwandtner's Wartime Knitting Circle installation.

homepage.mac.com/halfangel/ knitting-ie/theknittingmap.html
Home page for The Knitting Map.

www.arts.wisc.edu/artsinstitute/ air/morton/about.html
Web page featuring Janet Morton's works.

Felted Nest

Fine art knitalongs remind us it's okay to create things purely because they're cool or make us think about the world. Case in point: this felted nest. Maybe it makes you think about the notion of home. Or maybe it could be a nestlike spot for change, keys, fabric scraps, knitting tools, or needles. But mostly what it does is fascinate with its tiny roundness as it emerges from its third swish in a hot washing machine. Add ribbons, bows, and vintage appliqués, or make the basic model in a host of colors.

FINISHED MEASUREMENTS 16¹/₄" circumference at widest point, before felting; 15" after felting

YARN Brown Sheep Lamb's Pride Bulky (85% wool / 15% mohair; 125 yards / 4 ounces): Version 1: 1 skein #M175 Bronze Patina; Version 2: 1 skein #M191 Kiwi. Beaded version design by Elizabeth New.

NEEDLES One set of five double-pointed needles (dpn) size US 11 (8 mm); one 16" (40 cm) circular (circ) needle size US 11 (8 mm)

NOTIONS Stitch marker; removable marker (or safety pin). *For Version 2 only:* one 3-gram tube size 11 silver-lined transparent brown round Japanese seed beads; matching beading thread; size 12 beading needle; vintage iron-on bird appliqué (or iron-on fabric decal); pale pink embroidery floss

GAUGE Not essential for this project.

NOTES

You may want to carry along an additional yarn for a decorative effect, such as Habu Textiles Cork Chenille or a mohair loop yarn. Test additional yarns by knitting and felting a swatch first. Work pattern as written, without changing instructions for additional materials you hold together with the yarn.

NEST

With color of your choice, CO 18 sts; divide among 3 dpns. Join for working in the rnd, being careful not to twist sts; place

marker (pm) for beginning of rnd.

Rnd 1: *K3, m1; repeat from * around—24 sts.
Rnd 2 and All Even-Numbered Rnds: Knit.
Rnd 3: *K4, m1; repeat from * around—30 sts.
Rnd 5: *K6, m1; repeat from * around—35 sts.
Rnd 7: *K7, m1; repeat from * around—40 sts.
Rnd 9: *K5, m1; repeat from * around—48 sts. Place removable marker in last st of rnd.
Next Rnd: Change to circ needle; work even in St st for 6" from removable marker. Remove marker.

SHAPE NEST

Rnd 1: *K6, k2tog; repeat from * around—42 sts remain.
Rnds 2, 4, 6, and 8: Knit.
Rnd 3: *K4, k2tog; repeat from * around—35 sts remain.
Rnd 5: *K3, k2tog; repeat from * around—28 sts remain.
Rnd 7: *K1, k2tog; repeat from * to last st, k1—19 sts remain.
Rnd 9: *K1, k2tog; repeat from * to last st, k1—13 sts remain.
Rnd 10: *K2tog; repeat from * to last 3 sts, k3tog—6 sts remain.
Rnd 11: *K2tog; repeat from * around—3 sts remain. Cut yarn, leaving a 6" tail. Draw through remaining sts, pull tight and fasten off. Weave in end.

FINISHING

Wash Nest in a washing machine in hot water with a small amount of soap and a pair of jeans or a towel for friction. Repeat washing three or four times, until the Nest has reached the desired consistency and shape. Dry in a hot dryer and finish shaping by hand if desired.

Version 2 Embellishment

Cut out your chosen decal or appliqué. Rather than follow package instructions, simply sew the decal onto the Nest as follows. Separate 3 of the 6 strands of embroidery floss. Using beading needle and 3 strands of floss held together, sew decal in place where desired, varying the spacing between sts so several group together and overlap in some places. Secure floss and hide ends inside Nest.

Apply seed beads in a free-hand branch design, using a 3-bead back st, as follows: Thread beading thread through beading needle and knot it. Bring needle up through fabric from WS in desired location. Thread 3 beads onto needle and slide them to the opposite end. *Take needle back through fabric to WS in desired location, making sure beads are flush with fabric, not buckled or loose. Bring needle back to RS between last 2 beads, thread needle through last bead, thread 3 more beads on needle; repeat from * until design is complete, making two rnds of beads around opening. Secure ends inside Nest.

Chapter Four Growing

All knitters have room to grow and get better, whether they're just learning to purl or taking a stab at steeks or sophisticated entrelac.

And no matter what your personal challenge, there's probably someone somewhere running a knitalong that could help you face it—with a motivational mix of camaraderie, gentle peer pressure, and technical help. In this chapter, we'll explore three ways you might grow as a knitter from the experience of knitting along: through competition, technical challenges, and collaboration.

First, we look in on the scene at state fair knitting competitions. Behind the carnival midway and the cotton candy stands, you'll find a knitting meet-up with competitors you might never otherwise encounter, expert judges, and once in a while, cash prize money. It's an experience that inspired the Blue Ribbon Scrap Wrap. As the name implies, it was a winner.

New techniques can be scary to try, but they open up a whole new world of knitted possibilities. In that spirit, we look into challenge knitalongs like the Knitting Olympics—knitalongs with the goal of bringing out the Olympian in every participant—and match that story with two patterns that seem well worth a bit of stretching to achieve a new technique: the Entomology Hat and Mitten Set and the Eden Scarf.

Finally we look in on two collaborative celebrations where knitting is front and center. The "knittingway" is a special baby shower where everyone tests their skills. The Blessingway Blanket pattern was inspired by this type of knitalong, and it proves that challenging yourself to work up to the standards of a group gift is worth it when you've got a good reason and some lovely yarn. And the ultimate in knitted celebrations—not to mention an impressive knitting spectacle—must be a wedding in which every detail from dress to doves is knitted.

Competing at the State Fair

Nothing is quite the wonderland for a knitter as is the state fair. To begin with, you get to see the same attractions everyone else goes there for. Just inside the gates are Ferris wheels as big as interstate-highway cloverleafs, five different colors of cotton candy, deep-fried everything (Twinkies, candy bars, even, mysteriously, Coke), and shows by bands you thought had long since disbanded.

Winding your way back through the sideshows, you'll find the traditional heart of the fair: the livestock, to which knitters have an undeniable bond. The stalls and cages stretch out in epic lines, prize ribbons fluttering from the bars like eyelashes. Goats poke their heads through the bars with randy little nods, sheep shuffle and blink, and fat, fluffy rabbits don't seem to do much except sniff and look irresistibly soft. The knitter in you eyes each animal as though it were already a ball of yarn, and says a silent thank-you.

Leaving the stalls, you find the Home Arts pavilion—which just a few decades ago was probably called something like "Women's World." There, in rows, stacks, cabinets, and wall arrangements, are the pies, the pickles, the quilts, the thousand domestic challenges in which, once a year, you can compete for a blue ribbon.

As you angle in on the knitting displays, your heart beats like a drum. Where is your work? And does it have a ribbon?

"It's a really exciting experience," says Janita James, superintendent of the Home Arts competitions at the Oregon State Fair in Salem. Janita is herself the veteran of many competitions, and she sounds like she misses the fray more than a little bit.

Good-natured competition is an ancient part of the fair experience. In medieval times, merchants jostled for attention at yearly fairs at places like Champagne, France, and Stourbridge, England. By the America of the twentieth century, fairs were more limited in scope but every bit as essential to the people attending them. State fairs—and similar events like Royal Shows in Australia and the U.K., and provincial exhibitions in Canada—were primarily agricultural shows, places for farmers to meet, talk, learn, and promote their most impressive accomplishments.

Naturally, there were contests. Manly events like hog breeding and tractor pulls were soon joined by "womanly" ones. In states around the nation, people have been competing in the fields of preserves, pies, and quilts since the mid-1800s—meaning that today's knitting showdowns are part of a tradition a century-and-a-half old.

The number of knitting entries at American fairs slumped in the 1980s and 1990s, along with a general lull in the craft's popularity. But as knitting has skyrocketed to prominence again, fair competitions have gotten livelier, too. There's a breadth of styles and techniques that could shock you right before it gives you an epiphany. For instance, you might not think of knitting a purple pantsuit, but somebody did, and that knitter was proud enough of it to put it in the fair.

Should you throw your own hat (or scarf, or pantsuit) into the ring? Absolutely, says Janita. "It'll make you stretch to do things a little different or better," she says. "You want to put on a good show."

Being judged outright can be an odd experience for a first-time entrant. Judges might critique winning entries as well as those without ribbons, often placing a premium on execution and technique. Materials and colors must be appropriate, ends tucked in, tension regular, and finishing complete ("No knots, please!" or "Hat's crown not pulled tight enough" are typical judges' commentary). Depending on the fair, originality and design may or may not be a big part of the judges' scorecards.

In this scenario, coming home without a ribbon can teach you just as much as winning. Either way, by entering you've joined thousands of knitters past and present in a kind of knitalong that will help you grow as an artisan. Now head back to the midway and get yourself a congratulatory deep-fried Twinkie.

Finding a Fair

Visit these websites to locate a fair near you:

www.weekendevent.com/statefairs.htm

www.fairsnet.org

www.countyfairgrounds.net

www.breedersworld.com/fairs.html

www.canadian-fairs.ca

larissa's
THE FAIR-ALONG
Knitalong Diary

I love the State Fair and brave the hot family car to go every September. In 2005 I just had to attend, despite my worries about taking our tiny baby (as a first-time mother, I was afraid he would literally melt). We watched dog agility contests and Chinese acrobats, petted miniature goats, and lost ourselves in a fog of cotton candy. Martin even won me a stuffed animal! There was just one thing that wasn't quite what I'd expected it to be—the knitting.

I had entered the Home Arts competitions and was delighted to find I'd won—third place for a baby hat and second place for a handbag. There was some skilled and lovely knitting entered alongside mine, but as a first-time competitor I was surprised at how easy it was to break in. My felted bag had only *two* rivals. In fact, all of the knitting from the state of Oregon fit into a few display cases. Where were my peers, I wondered—women from the LYS (local yarn store) and the blogs? Where were the people I saw purling on the bus, my friends who knit with every free second, and the moms in my son's play group who'd been rediscovering and reshaping the domestic aesthetic of pies, lemonade, and of course, knitting? I wanted each of them to bring on the handknits.

I swore solemnly on my blog, "Next year I'm going on a campaign."

My dreams of storming the fair with a posse of knitters were forgotten as the sun hid behind a moody pastiche of Portland clouds. But in May, my vision came back to life. I started organizing locally and recruited a knitting café, Abundant Yarn & Dyeworks, to cohost a weekly drop-in knitalong. The shop recognized all joiners on a big chalkboard, and gave us a café discount.

Then, serendipity! Janita James, superintendent of the Home Arts competitions at the Oregon State Fair, visited Abundant Yarn and noticed our knitalong. She was so enthused she contributed free fair tickets. We were official.

Meanwhile, I couldn't restrain my enthusiasm to just one state fair. I wrote about my summer-hazy visions of people knitting and entering fairs all over the

world, and I started an Internet knitalong to complement my local effort.

A simple announcement on my blog invited anyone anywhere with dreams of entering his or her own fair competition to knit along with me. Signing up was as easy as leaving a comment. The deadline was the deadline of each participant's local fair. I asked Quiet Cricket—a user on Flickr.com—for permission to use her photo of jam jars, and I made a Fair-Along "button," an electronic logo with a link for the KAL. (As per blogging convention, those who used the button on their blogs made it link back to mine to help increase KAL sign-ups.) Every week I read dozens of blogs, then wrote on mine about everyone's progress. I wasn't the only one with fair fever. More than 50 people signed on.

"My husband's been trying to get me to enter the fair for years," wrote Janine from Oklahoma, "This may be just the thing to get me to stay on task!" Natalie, from California, wrote, "I am a solitary knitter. I'm itching to get out!"

As fall came and fair tents went up, our fair-alongers made a powerful mark. In Michigan, Beth took home ribbons for her shawl and handspun yarn. In Iowa, Meghan won two awards, despite some judges' critiques pinned to her items. Heidi got red ribbons on her gorgeous hat and mittens, and entered jam too, in the Kalamazoo County Fair. Here at home, Pat took the blue for an afghan, Hannah tied for second in the "fastest fingers" knitting contest, and Katrina won a blue ribbon for a silvery silk scarf.

As I approached the display cases on the day I visited the fair, my friend Sarah was already there, beaming. She'd won first place for Item of Original Design—a cabled cape made of silk and scraps of stash yarn. We've reproduced it here as the Blue Ribbon Scrap Wrap. You may enjoy working on it as you scheme up a strategy for next year's competition—hopefully, a heated one.

Blue Ribbon Scrap Wrap

This rich and luscious wrap, which won first prize at the Oregon State Fair, showcases a bit of hand-spun yarn mixed with Noro Silk Garden and other yarn scraps. Using a top-down raglan construction, the wrap follows a set of easily memorized guidelines for color changes and cable crosses.

DESIGN BY SARAH GILBERT

FINISHED MEASUREMENTS 57" circumference

YARN Noro Silk Garden (45% silk / 45% mohair / 10% wool; 110 yards / 50 grams): 2 hanks #084 (MC); Frog Tree Alpaca Wool (100% alpaca; 130 yards/1³/₄ oz): 1 skein #23 (A); 2 ounces thick handspun yarn to coordinate (B) (shown in handspun wool and silk spun by Kimberly Kern).
Note: In place of yarn A, you may use 120 yards of any coordinating light worsted-weight yarn(s). In place of B, you may use any yarn with which you can achieve the required gauge, such as Brown Sheep Lamb's Pride Bulky.

NEEDLES One circular (circ) needle size US 10¹/₂ (6.5 mm), any length; one pair straight needles size US 9 (5.5 mm). Change needle size if necessary to obtain correct gauge.

NOTIONS Stitch markers; cable needle (cn); row counter (optional); French cufflink or special button, approximately 1" across

GAUGE 14 sts and 22 rows = 4" (10 cm) in Stockinette stitch (St st) with larger needles and MC
12 sts and 14 rows = 4" (10 cm) in Stockinette stitch with larger needles and B

NOTES

Wrap is worked in one piece from the top down. On each row, you will work through five sections: Border, Shoulder, Back Panel, Shoulder, and Border. Work a 5-stitch Seed stitch border at the beginning and end of every row, and change yarn at the beginning of every WS row. When working the cable patterns, note that each pattern has a different row repeat.

Abbreviations

C4F: Slip 2 sts to cn, hold to front, k2, k2 from cn.
C5B: Slip 3 sts to cn, hold to back, k2, slip last st from cn back to left-hand needle, p1, k2 from cn.
C7B: Slip 4 sts to cn, hold to back, k3, slip last st from cn back to left-hand needle, p1, k3 from cn.

Seed Stitch

(multiple of 2 sts + 1; 1-row repeat)
All Rows: K1, *p1, k1; repeat from * to end.

4-Stitch Cable

(panel of 4 sts; 4-row repeat)
Row 1 (RS): Knit.
Row 2: Purl.
Row 3: C4F.
Row 4: Purl.
Repeat Rows 1-4 for 4-Stitch Cable.

5-Stitch Cable

(panel of 5 sts; 6-row repeat)
Rows 1 and 5 (RS): K2, p1, k2.
Rows 2 and 4: P2, k1, p1.
Row 3: C5B.
Row 6: Repeat Row 2.
Repeat Rows 1-6 for 5-Stitch Cable.

7-Stitch Cable

(panel of 7 sts; 10-row repeat)

Row 1 (RS): K3, p1, k3.

Rows 2, 4, 6 and 8: P3, k1, p3.

Rows 3, 5, and 7: K3, p1, k3.

Row 9: C7B.

Row 10: Repeat Row 2.

Repeat Rows 1-10 for 7-Stitch Cable.

Back Panel Pattern

(panel of 43 sts; 2-row repeat)

Row 1 (RS): P2, work 4-Stitch Cable, p1, work 5-Stitch Cable, p1, work 4-Stitch Cable, p1, work 7-Stitch Cable, p1, work 4-Stitch Cable, p1, work 5-Stitch Cable, p1, work 4-Stitch Cable, p2.

Row 2: K2, work 4-Stitch Cable, k1, work 5-Stitch Cable, k1, work 4-Stitch Cable, k1, work 7-Stitch Cable, k1, work 4-Stitch Cable, k1, work 5-Stitch Cable, k1, work 4-Stitch Cable, k2.

Repeat Rows 1 and 2 for Back Panel Pattern.

WRAP

Note: Unless otherwise instructed, do NOT cut yarn. Carry yarn not in use up outside edge.

Using larger needle and B, CO 81 sts.

Row 1 (RS): Set row counter at 1. Work 5 sts in Seed st, place marker (pm) for right Shoulder, work in St st (beginning with knit) for 14 sts, pm for Back Panel, work Back Panel Pattern over 43 sts, pm for left Shoulder, work in St st (beginning with knit) for 14 sts, pm for Border, work in Seed st to end.

Row 2: Change to MC. Work even for 1 row.

Row 3: Work to first marker, slip marker (sm), m1, work to last marker, m1, sm, work to end–83 sts.

Row 4: Change to B. Work even for 1 row, working increased sts in St st.

Row 5: Repeat Row 3–85 sts.

Rows 6-13: Repeat Rows 2-5–93 sts after Row 13. Cut B after Row 13.

Rows 14 and 15: Repeat Rows 2 and 3–95 sts.

Row 16: Change to A. Work even for 1 row.

Row 17: Repeat Row 3–97 sts.

Rows 18-29: Repeat Rows 14-17–109 sts after Row 29.

*Note: Continue changing colors as established: * work [2*

*rows MC, 2 rows B] 3 times, [2 rows MC, 2 rows A] 4 times; repeat from * for color sequence.*

Row 30: Repeat Row 14.

Row 31: Work to first marker, m1-p, sm, work to last marker, sm, m1-p, work to end–111 sts.

Row 32: Work 5 sts, k1, work to last 6 sts, k1, work to end.

Row 33: Work 5 sts, m1-p, p1, work to last marker, sm, p1, m1-p, work to end–113 sts.

Row 34: Work 5 sts, k2, work to last 7 sts, k2, work to end.

Row 35: Work 5 sts, m1, p2, work to last 7 sts, p2, m1, work to end–115 sts.

Row 36: Work 5 sts, p1, k2, work to last 8 sts, k2, p1, work to end.

Row 37: Work 5 sts, m1, k1, p2, work to last 8 sts, p2, k1, m1, work to end–117 sts.

Row 38: Work 5 sts, p2, k2, work to last 9 sts, k2, p2, work to end.

Row 39: Work 5 sts, m1, k2, p2, work to last 9 sts, p2, k2, m1, work to end–119 sts.

Row 40: Work 5 sts, p3, k2, work to last 10 sts, k2, p3, work to end.

Row 41: Work 5 sts, m1, k3, p2, work to last 10 sts, p2, k3, m1, work to end–121 sts.

Row 42: Work 5 sts, p4, k2, work to last 11 sts, k2, p4, work to end.

Row 43: Work 5 sts, m1, work 4-Stitch Cable, beginning on same row as Cable in back Panel, p2, work to last 11 sts, p2, work 4-Stitch Cable, beginning on same row as Cable in back Panel, m1, work to end–123 sts.

Row 44: Repeat Row 32.

Row 45: Work 5 sts, m1, p1, work to last 6 sts, p1, m1, work to end–125 sts.

Row 46: Work 5 sts, p1, k1, work to last 7 sts, k1, p1, work to end.

Row 47: Work 5 sts, m1, k1, p1, work to last 7 sts, p1, k1, m1, work to end–127 sts.

Row 48: Work 5 sts, p2, k1, work to last 8 sts, k1, p2, work to end.

Row 49: Work 5 sts, m1, k2, p1, work to last 8 sts, p1, k2, m1, work to end–129 sts.

Row 50: Work 5 sts, p3, k1, work to last 9 sts, k1, p3, work to end.

Row 51: Work 5 sts, m1, k3, p1, work to last 9 sts, p1, k3, m1, work to end–131 sts.

Row 52: Work 5 sts, p4, k1, work to last 10 sts, k1, p4, work to end.

Row 53: Work 5 sts, m1-p, work 4-Stitch Cable, beginning on same row as neighboring Cable, p1, work to last 10 sts, p1, work 4-Stitch Cable, beginning on same row as neighboring Cable, m1-p, work to end–133 sts.

Rows 54-73: Repeat Rows 44-53–153 sts.

Rows 74-76: Repeat Rows 32-34–155 sts after Row 75.

Work even until piece measures 19", or to desired length from the beginning, ending with a WS row and A.

Increase Row 1 (RS): Change to B and St st, continuing to work 5 sts at beginning and end of every row in Seed st. Work 5 sts, k1, m1, *k6, m1; repeat from * to last 5 sts, work to end–180 sts. Work even for 1 row.

Increase Row 2: Work 5 sts, k4, m1, *k6, m1; repeat from * to last 9 sts, k4, work to end–208 sts. Work even for 2 rows. BO all sts. Weave in all ends.

FINISHING

Closure: With RS facing, beginning just above CO edge, with smaller needles and 1 strand each of MC and B held together, pick up and knit 5 sts in first 5 rows of left Front Border. Begin Seed st. Work even for 16 rows.

Eyelet Row: K1, p1, yo, p2tog, k1.

Next Row: Work in Seed st. Work even for 1 row. BO all sts.

Sew button to opposite edge of Wrap, 3 rows below CO edge. If using French cufflink, insert through buttonhole without sewing.

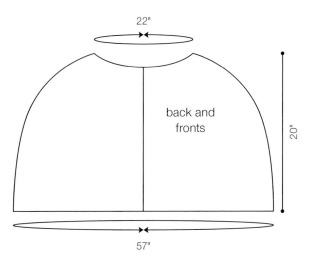

Note: Piece is worked from the top down.

Challenge Knitalongs

The Knitting Olympics started like a lot of other Internet knitalongs. A blogger was sitting in the glow of her computer screen, musing—in this case—about the upcoming Winter Olympics in Torino, Italy. She loved the Games and the idea of striving for a personal challenge. But she was no luge champion or power skater. How could she compete?

"I started thinking that knitting was my sport," says Stephanie Pearl-McPhee, known online as the Yarn Harlot. She wanted to knit something of Olympic difficulty during the games, and she thought other people might like to do this, too. So she typed out an invitation to the world of knitters: join her 2006 Knitting Olympics and embody the spirit of *Citius*, *Altius*, *Fortius*—faster, higher, stronger. Her "knitathletes" would be anyone else in the world who was willing to take on a challenging knitting project, and

cast on and finish entirely within the duration of the Torino Olympics: sixteen days from opening ceremonies to flame-snuffing.

There wasn't a whole lot of glamour to it, compared to the Torino games themselves. In the Knitting Olympics, participants got their names (and blog addresses, if they had them) on a list on the Yarn Harlot's site. If they completed their self-appointed task, they got the right to grab a digital picture of a gold medal to use on their own websites. There were no sponsorships or athletes' villages. No cascade of knitters came skiing past your house at night, candles in hand, on the eve of cast-on.

Nonetheless, 4,107 knitters responded—or about 1,600 more participants than there were athletes in Torino. Knitters formed teams and published online banners on their websites, based on country of origin (Team

Finland), knitting project type (The U.S. Cable Team), or performance-enhancement drug (Team Caffeine). As humble as Stephanie's initial intention may have been, the Knitting Olympics made news in the major media, like *Time* magazine.

The Knitting Olympics was the "perfect storm" of knitalongs—where a confluence of factors created an event as undeniable as a tidal wave. Once Stephanie put forth her initial idea on her blog, she says, "it spread like a virus."

Why was the Knitting Olympics such a watershed moment in online knitalongs, a defining point that thousands of knitters can remember participating in, much like others remember Woodstock?

It was a standard Internet challenge knitalong in a lot of ways. Stephanie called on knitters to finish a project in a specific time frame. Other knitalongs in this mode have included Summer of Lace, in which knitters challenged themselves with intricate holey patterns, Lint for Lent, which challenged knitters to knit a charity project during the six weeks before Easter, and Knit From Your Stash 2007, which challenged knitters to avoid the LYS (local yarn store) for most of that year, if they could stand it (one fall off the wagon was allowed).

Signing up for the Knitting Olympics gave participants a dollop of fame—their names and website links were entered on a list of participants, which doubled as a way for knitters to find each other's blogs, brag about their progress, and ask questions about tricky spots. Many online knitalongs have been structured this way, as a big list of links to participants' websites.

To motivate knitalongers, the Knitting Olympics offered prizes for a few finishers picked at random. Prizes were sometimes small but always motivational: a skein of something really exotic, maybe, or a set of handmade stitch markers. The digitial "gold medal" was a simple perk that was charming enough to make knitters around the world tuck in those final yarn ends.

Within this typical framework, the Knitting Olympics had several advantages. The Yarn Harlot was already a singularly popular blogger, with thousands of visitors to her site per day, before she started her knitalong. But other aspects of the event were clever choices that any blogger could adopt for his or her own KAL.

The challenge—to take on and finish a serious project—was clear, and yet easily adaptable for knitters with varying skills. While most knitalongs have more limitations, the flexibility of the Knitting Olympics made it ultimately "joinable" and made the results all the more fun and diverse. Says Stephanie, "While people were obviously part of a bigger movement, which is pretty empowering on its own, the successes that people were achieving were deeply personal."

The time frame and deadline for the Knitting Olympics were crystal clear, and short enough to focus attention. While not every knitalong has a global quadrennial sporting event to provide a built-in deadline, the most successful keep timeframes manageable and motivational. For example, a gift-along might be most successful in the last month before the holidays, but not if it spans the last ten months.

Finally, the Knitting Olympics was tied to something big and inspirational: the real Olympic Games. While knitting certainly is its own reward, it can be extra motivational to put it in a bigger context. (It only added to the perfection of this knitalong that the Olympics happen to be an event that you watch for days and days while sitting on the couch, primed to knit.) Other knitalongs may find their context in charitable causes, seasons of the year, or in the nation's political calendar.

The result was a knitalong that marked a pivotal moment in the current revival of knitting, when the groundswell of Internet knitters that had been growing for years suddenly got organized enough to be visible to the rest of the world. It brought out a lot of knitters who felt misunderstood or embarrassed. "My husband says knitting makes me seem too grandmotherly," says one anonymous knitter. Another, known online only as teaandcakes, wrote on her blog, "Above is a picture of my bag. Inside my bag are needles and yarn, waiting to become wristwarmers. I'm in a café.

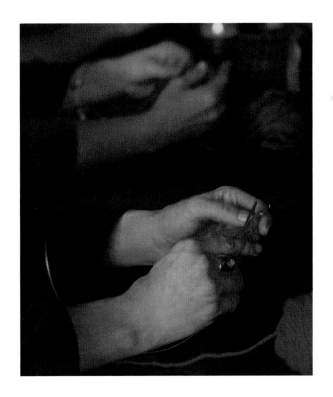

Olympian Challenges

Visit these websites for more information:

www.yarnharlot.ca
The Yarn Harlot's blog.
She plans to do other Knitting
Olympics for future Winter games.

www.olympic.org
The official website of the Olympic
Movement, which includes a history
of the Games since 1859
and news about future Games.

www.craftster.org/forum
A discussion board where you can
participate in monthly knitting challenges.

By myself. And I'm embarrassed to get them out and start knitting." The Knitting Olympics made knitters like these feel less alone.

"The Yarn Harlot's Knitting Olympics was a huge event to me," says Kathy, a knitter whose move to Alaska had left her without a LYS or knitting circle. "I really began to feel like I was part of a knitting community again, like a void was being filled." The Knitting Olympics made them part of something so big other people simply had to take notice.

For her part, McPhee has no problem being confi-dent and forthright about her knitting. But even she was surprised by the response to her invitation.

"Never in my wildest imagination (and for the record, my imagination is pretty wild)," wrote the Harlot on her blog, "did I imagine thousands upon thousands of knitters sending me an e-mail, thousands leaving comments, thou-sands latched on to the simple idea of striving to meet a personal challenge."

And never did so many knitters have so many reasons to feel like champions.

Entomology Hat & Mitten Set

If you're looking for a knitting challenge with immediate, amazing rewards, stranded colorwork could be just the thing. There's something magical about the first time you watch a motif take shape stitch by stitch, row by row, like dots in a Seurat masterpiece or cells in an Atari game, circa 1979. Whether you're spreading your wings for the first time or you've done colorwork for years, this delicious hat and mitten set tempts you with a motif unlike any traditional snowflake or deer. DESIGN BY ADRIAN BIZILIA

FINISHED MEASUREMENTS Mittens: 8^1/$_2$" circumference x 10^1/$_4$" long; Hat: 21" circumference (to fit average adult woman)

YARN Dale of Norway Falk (100% pure new wool; 116 yards / 50 grams): Mittens: 2 skeins #3072 Cocoa (MC), 1 skein #9725 Citron (A); Hat: 2 skeins #3072 Cocoa (MC), 1 skein #9725 Citron (A)

NEEDLES One set of five double-pointed needles (dpn) size US 1 (2.25 mm); one set of five double-pointed needles size US 3 (3.25 mm); one 16" (40 cm) circular (circ) needle size US 1 (2.25 mm); one 16" (40 cm) circular needle size US 3 (3.25 mm)

NOTIONS Stitch markers; waste yarn

GAUGE 26 sts and 28 rows = 4" (10 cm) in Stockinette stitch (St st) over Chart A using larger needles

NOTES

You may work a palm with or without the year. To work the palm without the year, simply work Chart B as given. To work the year into one or both palms, work Chart C within the green outline on Chart B.

Right Braid

Rnd 1: Holding both strands in front of work, and bringing the working strand under the non-working strand for each st, *p1 with MC, p1 with A; repeat from * around.

Rnd 2: Holding both strands in front of work, and bringing the working strand over the non-working strand for each st, *p1 with MC, p1 with A; repeat from * around.

Left Braid

Rnd 1: Holding both strands in front of work, and bringing the working strand over the non-working strand for each st, *p1 with MC, p1 with A; repeat from * around.

Rnd 2: Holding both strands in front of work, and bringing the working strand under the non-working strand for each st, *p1 with MC, p1 with A; repeat from * around.

MITTENS

Right Mitten

With smaller dpn and MC, CO 56 sts; divide among 4 dpn. Join for working in the rnd, being careful not to twist sts; place marker (pm) for beginning of rnd.

Note: If you prefer not to work the Braid, skip Rnds 1-3 and begin with Rnd 4.

Rnd 1: *K1 with MC, k1 with A; repeat from * around.

Rnds 2 and 3: Work Rnds 1 and 2 of Right Braid.

Rnd 4: Work 28 sts from Chart A, pm, work 28 sts from Chart B. Work even through Rnd 12 of Charts.

Rnd 13: Change to larger needles. Work even through Rnd 31 of Charts.

THUMB OPENING

Next Rnd: Work 31 sts, change to waste yarn, knit 12 sts, slip these 12 sts back to left-hand needle, change to working yarn, work these 12 sts again, working from Chart, work to end. Work even until Chart is complete, working decreases as indicated–12 sts remain. Cut yarn, leaving 6" tails. Thread both tails through remaining sts, pull tight and fasten off.

THUMB

Carefully remove waste yarn from Thumb sts and place bottom 12 sts and top 11 sts onto 2 larger dpns, being careful not to twist sts. Rejoin yarn to bottom sts. Begin Right Thumb Chart from Chart B, pick up 1 st at side of Thumb Opening and work together with first st on first needle, work across bottom sts; at side of Thumb Opening with second needle, pick up and knit 1 st, work across top sts–24 sts. *Note: You will work 2 repeats of Thumb Chart; 1 repeat across the bottom sts and 1 repeat across the top sts.* Redistribute sts evenly among 3 dpns. Join for working in the rnd; pm for beginning of rnd. Work even until Thumb Chart is complete, working decreases as indicated–8 sts remain. Cut yarn, leaving 6" tails. Thread both tails through remaining sts, pull tight and fasten off.

Left Mitten

Work as for Right Mitten, working Left Braid instead of Right Braid, and working Thumb Opening as follows:

THUMB OPENING

Next Rnd: Work 44 sts, change to waste yarn, knit 12 sts, slip these 12 sts back to left-hand needle, change to working yarn, work these 12 sts again, working from Chart, work to end. Complete as for Right Mitten, working Left Thumb Chart from Chart B instead of Right Thumb Chart.

FINISHING

Weave in all ends. Block Mittens.

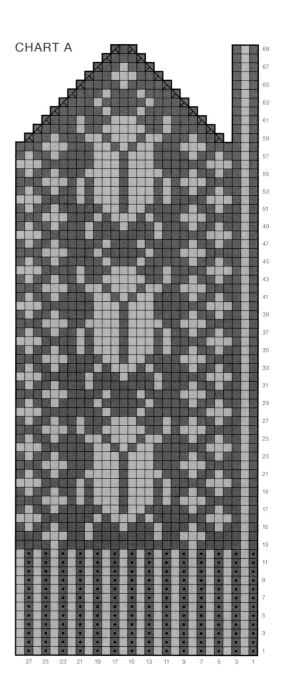

CHART A

CHART B

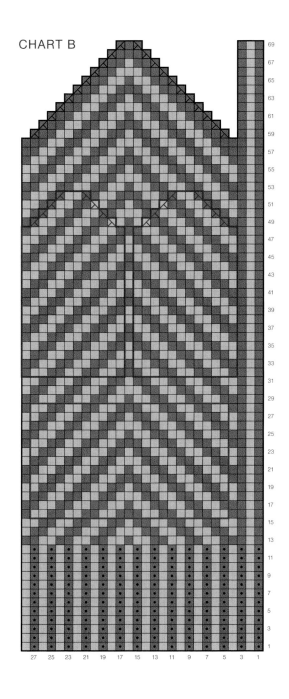

CHART C

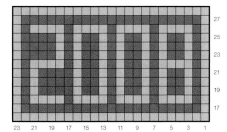

KEY

☐	Knit	☒	Ssk
•	Purl	▎	Work Chart C
■	MC	▎	Work Thumb
▨	A	☒	K2tog-worked on Thumb only.
☒	K2tog	☒	Ssk-worked on Thumb only.

CHART NOTES

Chart B includes right and left Thumb charts, outlined in red. To work the Thumb, follow instructions for picking up Thumb sts, then work the appropriate Thumb Chart, repeating the Thumb Chart once as you work around the Thumb.

Chart C is for the year, which you may add, if you choose, to the palm of one or both Mittens, in the area outlined in green.

HAT

Note: Change to dpns when necessary for number of sts on needle.

With smaller circ needle and MC, CO 132 sts. Join for working in the rnd, being careful not to twist sts; pm for beginning of rnd. *Note: If you prefer not to work the Braid, skip Rnds 1-3, and start with the Lining, as follows: Work in St st for 2", purl 1 rnd (turning rnd), knit 1 rnd, then proceed to Rnd 4.*

Rnd 1: *K1 with MC, k1 with A; repeat from * around.

Rnds 2 and 3: Work Rnds 1 and 2 of Left Braid.

Rnd 4: Change to larger circ needle. Begin Chart D. Work even until Chart is complete.

Next Rnd: Change to Chart E, working decreases as indicated in Chart–8 sts remain. Cut yarn, leaving a 6" tail. Thread through remaining sts, pull tight and fasten off. *Note: If you skipped the Braid and began with the Lining, sew CO edge of lining to WS of Hat, being careful not to let sts show on RS.*

Lining

Note: Omit these instructions if you began the Hat by working the Lining. With RS facing and Hat held upside-down, with smaller circ needles and MC, pick up and knit 132 sts through back loops of CO row. Join for working in the rnd; pm for beginning of rnd. Begin St st. Work even for 2". BO all sts very loosely. Cut yarn, leaving a 1 yard tail. Sew BO edge to WS of Hat, being careful not to let sts show on RS.

FINISHING

Weave in all ends. Block Hat.

CHART E

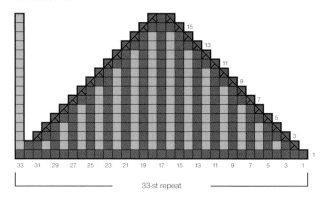

33-st repeat

CHART D

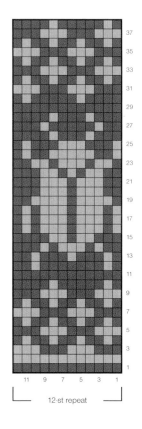

12-st repeat

Eden Scarf

Have you ever hiked on a green forested path or strolled along a windy shoreline and thought, I want to knit something that beautiful? It's probably impossible to create something as breathtaking as nature itself, but as knitters we often yearn to try. This scarf is one more attempt at grace. It's also an opportunity to learn new techniques on a small scale. Experiment with color, yarn choice, and leaf and blossom placement. And beware: Everyone who sees this scarf will ask you to make them one.

FINISHED MEASUREMENTS Version 1 (Brown): 54" long; Version 2 (Ivory): 48" long. Length will vary depending on leaf placement; each leaf should measure approximately 3" long.

YARN ShibuiKnits Merino Kid (55% kid mohair / 45% merino wool; 218 yards / 100 grams): Version 1: 1 hank #MK7533 Bark (MC); Version 2: 1 hank #MK7501 Ivory (MC); ShibuiKnits Sock (100% superwash merino wool; 191 yards / 50 grams): Version 1: 1 hank #S220 Peony (A); Version 2: 1 hank #S402 Sand (A)
Note: Each Blossom uses approximately 4 yards, or 1 gram, of sock or fingering weight yarn. If you wish, experiment with making Blossoms out of leftover yarn you have in your stash.

NEEDLES One pair double-pointed needles (dpn) size US 7 (4.5 mm); one pair double-pointed needles size US 1½ (2.5 mm). Change needle size if necessary to obtain correct gauge.

NOTIONS
One yard waste yarn; straight pins for blocking

GAUGE
20 sts and 25 rows = 4" (10 cm) in Stockinette stitch (St st) using larger needles and MC

Abbreviations

Dvw (double vertical wrap): Bring yarn forward between the two needles, down the front of the work, and wrap under the bottom of the work. Come up the back and through the needles again to wrap a second time, ending with yarn in the back, ready to knit the next st. Be sure to knit the next st snugly to pull the wraps tight.

SCARF
First Half of Scarf
With larger needles and waste yarn, CO 3 sts.

STEM
Change to MC and I-Cord (see page 156). Work even for 15 rows. Do NOT turn work; slide sts to opposite end of needle and bring yarn around behind work to right-hand side, ready to work another RS row. Begin working a Leaf.

LEAF
Row 1 (RS): K1, m1, k1, m1, k1–5 sts.
Row 2 and all WS Rows: Purl.
Row 3: K1, m1, k3, m1, k1–7 sts.
Row 5: K1, m1, k2, m1, k1, m1, k2, m1, k1–11 sts.
Rows 7 and 9: Knit.
Row 11: K2, skp, k3, k2tog, k2–9 sts remain.
Row 13: K2, skp, k1, k2tog, k2–7 sts remain.
Row 15: K2, dcd, k2–5 sts remain.
Row 17: K1, dcd, k1–3 sts remain.
Row 19: Dcd–1 st remains. Cut yarn, leaving a 3-4" tail. Draw through remaining stitch, pull tight and fasten off.

STEM AND LEAF

*Holding the finished Leaf pointing away from you, and starting about 1" up the Stem from where the Leaf body begins, pick up 3 sts without knitting them (simply put them on your needle). Join MC, leaving a 4" tail. Work I-Cord for 11 rows, carrying the tail up inside the I-Cord. Work Rows 1-19 of Leaf. Repeat from * 16 times (you will have 18 Leaves). *Note: Vary where you pick up the 3 sts on the Stem, to make the Leaves branch off in different directions.*

Second Half of Scarf

Carefully remove waste yarn from beginning of First Half of Scarf and place the 3 sts on larger needle. Work as for First Half of Scarf.

Blossoms (make 3 or 5)

With smaller needles and A, CO 30 sts.
Rows 1 and 3: Knit.
Rows 2 and 4: Purl.
Row 5: K3, dvw, *k6, dvw; repeat from * to last 3 sts, k3.
Row 6: *P2tog; repeat from * to end–15 sts remain.
Row 7: *K2tog; repeat from * to last st, k1–8 sts remain.
Row 8: *P2tog; repeat from * to end–4 sts remain.
Row 9: [K2tog] twice, pass first st over last st and off the needle–1 st remains. Cut yarn, leaving an 8" tail. Draw through remaining st, pull tight and fasten off. Using tapestry needle and tail, sew sides of Blossom together.

FINISHING

Trim any remaining Stem tails. Weave in all ends.
Fill in any sparse spots with 4 to 6 additional leaves around the neck area, by working a Stem and Leaf at each spot.
Sew Blossoms to Scarf in small clusters, asymmetrically, and weave in any ends.
Block Scarf by pinning each Leaf out with 3 pins, 2 at the widest part of the Leaf and one at the point. Pin Blossoms to block, if desired. Spray with water and let dry completely.
Note: On both Leaves and Blossoms, some curling around the edges is desirable.

Collaborative Knitalongs

On a crisp, sunny afternoon in 2006, in a house on a lovely tree-lined street, a baby shower was getting underway. It was traditional in many ways—the table was set with hot tea and tiny sandwiches, the floor teemed with infants and toddlers winding their ways through the feet of a dozen moms. But when it came down to the games and activities, this shower was different. It was a "knittingway."

All across the United States, women are trying out a new alternative to baby showers called a blessingway. Inspired by a Navajo ceremony of the same name, a birth blessingway is part party, part ritual. It honors and supports the mother-to-be with wishes for strength and wisdom. Instead of showering her with tiny clothes and towering diaper cakes, women at a blessingway give her foot baths, hand massages, and stories. They create a sacred space to help ease the transition into motherhood.

Often a ball of yarn is passed around. Each guest ties a piece to his or her wrist, and wears the bracelet until the baby is born.

In the case of the knittingway, the shared yarn experience went much further. The mom-to-be was engineer Shetha Nolke, an avid knitter. Her friends concocted a fibery twist on the blessingway. Each guest knitted a cabled strip out of vividly colored Noro Silk Garden yarn. At the party, everyone brought their work with them and performed a binding-off ceremony full of well wishes and blessings for Shetha and her baby-to-be. Shetha's mother and mother-in-law were there to work some of the final stitches in the strips. Later, a couple of friends took the strips home and mattress-stitched them into a triangular shawl for Shetha to use right away, and for baby Gabriel to use as a blanket once he came into the world.

"It was so moving to see everyone knitting together that afternoon," says Shetha's friend Erica, who did not know until then that some of her friends could knit. "Just seeing everyone knitting made me feel so at home with my friends. It made knowing how to knit seem as natural as breathing."

Childbirth might be the rite of passage most indelibly linked to knitting (baby booties have been around for centuries), but it doesn't have to be the only one. Rachael Matthews of the London-based Cast Off Knitting Club mounted a "knitted wedding" (picture on page 31). It was a modest notion at first. Rachael's initial idea was to do a piece of performance art, a *pretend* wedding where everything—from dress to cake to corsage to the tin cans on the honeymoon vehicle—was knitted. Accordingly, she sent out 1,000 "invitations" to knit for or attend the event. Word got around, and she ultimately coordinated the labors of well over 500 people.

"We kept saying it was a performance," Rachael recalls, "but then we realized that everybody involved was slightly scared. Everybody was worried—would everything get knitted on time? Would the wedding be all right? Would the bride turn up? All the same sorts of emotions that you'd have with a normal wedding."

When the event finally came there were bridesmaids in knitted dresses, hundreds of guests, and, from out of nowhere, real paparazzi photographers. The couple "performing" as the bride and groom—artists Freddie Robins and Ben Coode-Adams—looked suitably shining and dumbstruck. They were already legally married, but this event was a far cry from their dry and minimal town-hall ceremony, and they couldn't help but enjoy it.

It turned out, says Rachael, "it wasn't possible to have a pretend wedding. If you have two people in love, and you say it's a wedding, then it's a wedding." Of course, hundreds of knitted flowers didn't hurt the atmosphere at all.

The blessingway and wedding projects show that knitting collaborations often result in more than just finished objects. Participating can push you to try new techniques, venture into new territory, and revel in doing good work with your peers. You might try a lace pattern you hadn't considered before or rekindle a lost love of cabling.

Knitting along might even encourage a friend who's a real beginner to spread her knitting wings. "I love Hau's piece," Shetha says of one friend who worked a plain Stockinette portion of Shetha's knittingway blanket even though it was a large piece of work for such a newbie. "She doesn't call herself a knitter, and yet she did it anyway. That's very meaningful to me."

When you venture to coordinate or assemble a collaborative project, you could grow further, as an artist and problem solver. The variety that results when different people knit, even from the same pattern and yarn, can give collaborative projects their character and charm— but it can also lead to difficulty integrating various knitters' work. Sewing together a collaborative blanket, you might struggle to find the right layout for three dozen variably colored squares (none of which exactly measures the nine square inches called for by the pattern). And you certainly will develop strong feelings for mattress or whip stitch.

Perhaps, like Rachael, you'll discover something you never really knew about human impulses toward celebration and romance. Collaborating on a really special gift means working with other knitters on a deadline, in

Collaboration

To learn more, visit these websites:

www.blessingwaybook.com
Provides some basic information on the blessingway trend and promotes the book *Mother Rising: The Blessingway Journey into Motherhood.*

www.knittinghelp.com
Provides free online videos of maneuvers used in assembling pieces for collaborative projects, such as mattress stitch, Kitchener stitch, and more.

www.castoff.info/wedding.asp
Experience Cast Off's Knitted Wedding, complete with free patterns for knitted candles, doves, and sandwiches, and photo galleries of the event.

a spirit of generosity. It can spark new relationships, or make you fall in love with your old friends all over again.

The icing on the cake is how the recipient feels about the unique gift. Shetha's baby, Gabriel, likes the weight of the blanket swaddled around him; his mom appreciates it differently. "I think about the blessings in this blanket when I wrap Gabriel in it," says Shetha. "I think about how cool it was that people from all parts of my life took part in it. My sister-in-law, my mother, and my mother-in-law all knitted these stitches. There's an aura about it I can't explain."

Blessingway Blanket

This blanket draws on the practice of the baby blessingway. Its five sections offer a perfect way for knitters of varying abilities to collaborate and deliver their best wishes. DESIGN BY HANNAH CUVIELLO

FINISHED MEASUREMENTS 35" square after finishing

YARN Blue Sky Alpacas Organic Cotton (100% organic cotton; 150 yards / 100 grams): 8 hanks #82 Nut

NEEDLES One 24" (60 cm) circular (circ) needle, size US 9 (5.5 mm). Change needle size if necessary to obtain correct gauge.

NOTIONS Stitch markers; cable needle (cn); removable markers

GAUGE 16 sts and 20 rows = 4" (10 cm) in Stockinette stitch (St st)

Seed Stitch
(multiple of 2 sts + 1; 1-row repeat)
All Rows: K1, *p1, k1; repeat from * to end.

BLANKET
Piece A (make 2)–Advanced
CO 2 sts.
SHAPE PIECE
Setup Row (WS): [K1-f/b] twice–4 sts.
Row 1 (RS): K4.
Row 2: K1, p2, k1.
Row 3: K1, m1-p, k2, m1-p, k1–6 sts.
Row 4: K1, p4, k1.
Row 5: K1, p1, m1, k2, m1, p1, k1–8 sts.
Row 6: K1, p1, k1, p2, k1, p1, k1.
Row 7: K1, p1, k1, m1-p, k2, m1-p, k1, p1, k1–10 sts.
Row 8: K1, p1, k1, p4, k1, p1, k1.
Row 9: [K1, p1] twice, m1, k2, m1, [p1, k1] twice–12 sts.
Row 10: [K1, p1] 3 times, [p1, k1] 3 times.
Row 11: Work 5 sts in Seed st as established, place marker

(pm), k1-f/b, m1-p, k1, pm, work in Seed st to end–14 sts.
Row 12: Work in Seed st to first marker, p1, knit to 1 st before next marker, p1, work in Seed st to end.
Row 13: Work to first marker, k1, m1-p, purl 1 st before next marker, m1-p, k1, work to end–16 sts.
Rows 14-33: Repeat Rows 12-13–36 sts after Row 33.
Row 34: Work to first marker, p1, work across Chart A to 1 st before next marker, p1, work to end.
Row 35: Work to first marker, k1, m1-p, work to 1 st before next marker, m1-p, k1, work to end–38 sts.
Rows 36-97: Repeat Rows 34 and 35, working increased sts into chart as they become available–100 sts after Row 97.
Row 98: Repeat Row 34.
Row 99: Change to Seed st, discontinuing increases.
Rows 100-102: Work even in Seed st. BO all sts in pattern.

Piece B–Adventurous Beginner
CO 2 sts.
Row 1 (RS): K1, p1.
Row 2: P1, k1.
SHAPE PIECE
Row 3: K1, p1-f/b–3 sts.
Row 4: K1, p1, k1.
Row 5: K1, p1, k1-f/b–4 sts.
Row 6: [P1, k1] twice.
Row 7: K1, p1, k1, p1-f/b–5 sts.
Row 8: [K1, p1] twice, k1.
Row 9: [K1, p1] twice, k1-f/b–6 sts.
Row 10: [P1, k1] 3 times.
Row 11: [K1, p1] twice, k1, p1-f/b–7 sts.
Row 12: [K1, p1] 3 times, k1.
Row 13: K1, p1, k1, m1, [p1, k1] twice–8 sts.
Row 14: [K1, p1] twice, k2, p1, k1.

Row 15: K1, p1, k1, pm, m1, pm, [k1, p1] twice, k1–9 sts.

Row 16: [K1, p1] 4 times, k1.

Row 17: Work in Seed st to first marker, k1, m1, sm, work in Seed st as established to end–10 sts.

Row 18: Work to first marker, p2, work to end.

Row 19: Work to first marker, k1, m1-p, k1, work to end–11 sts.

Row 20: Work to first marker, p1, k1, p1, work to end.

Row 21: Work to first marker, k1, p1, m1-p, k1, work to end–12 sts.

Row 22: Work to first marker, p1, k2, p1, work to end.

Rows 23, 25, 27, 29, 31, and 33: Work in Seed st to first marker, k1, purl to 1 st before next marker, m1-p, k1, work in Seed st to end–18 sts after Row 33.

Rows 24, 26, 28, 30, 32, and 34: Work to first marker, knit the knit sts and purl the purl sts to next marker, work to end.

Rows 35, 37, 39, 41, 43, and 45: Work to 1 st before second marker, m1, work to end–24 sts after Row 45.

Rows 36, 38, 40, 42, 44, and 46: Work to first marker, purl to 9 sts before next marker, k8, p1, work to end.

BEGIN CHART

Row 47: Work in Seed st to first marker, k1, p8, k6, m1-p, k1, work in Seed st to end–25 sts.

Row 48 and all WS Rows Through Row 60: Repeat Row 24.

Row 49: Work in Seed st to first marker, k1, work st #s 1-15 from Chart B, purl to 1 st before next marker, m1-p, k1, work in Seed st to end–26 sts.

Note: On following rows, work 1 additional st from Chart before each increased stitch.

Rows 49, 51, 53, 55, and 57: Work in Seed st to first marker, k1, work across Chart to 1 st before next marker, m1-p, k1, work in Seed st to end–30 sts after Row 57.

Row 59: Work to 1 st before second marker, m1-p, k1, work to last 2 sts, p2tog.

Row 61: Work to 1 st before second marker, m1-p, k1, work to last 2 sts, k2tog.

Row 62: Repeat Row 48. Place removable marker at beginning of row.

Row 63: Work to first marker, work across Chart to second marker, work to end. Work even until piece measures approximately 26" from removable marker, ending with Row 2 of Chart.

SHAPE PIECE

Row 1: Work to 3 sts before second marker, p2tog, work to last st, k1-f/b.

Row 2 and all WS Rows: Work even as established.

Row 3: Work to 3 sts before second marker, p2tog, work to last st, p1-f/b.

Rows 5, 7, 9, 11, 13, 27, 29, 31, 33, 35, 37, 39, and 41: Work to 3 sts before second marker, p2tog, work to end–11 sts remain after Row 41.

Rows 15, 17, 19, 21, 23, and 25: Work to 3 sts before second marker, k2tog, work to end–19 sts remain after Row 25.

Row 43: Work to first marker, k2tog, work to end–10 sts remain.

Row 45: K1, p1, k2tog, work to end–9 sts remain.

Rows 47, 51, and 55: Work to last 2 sts, k2tog–6 sts remain after Row 55.

Rows 49, 53, and 57: Work to last 2 sts, p2tog–3 sts remain after Row 57.

Row 58: Work even as established. BO all sts.

Piece C–Advanced

CO 2 sts.

SHAPE PIECE

Setup Row (WS): [K1-f/b] twice–4 sts.

Row 1 (RS): K4.

Row 2: K1, p2, k1.

Row 3: K1, m1-p, k2, m1-p, k1–6 sts.

Row 4: K1, p4, k1.

Row 5: K1, p1, m1, k2, m1, p1, k1–8 sts.

Row 6: K1, p1, k1, p2, k1, p1, k1.

Row 7: K1, p1, k1, m1-p, k2, m1-p, k1, p1, k1–10 sts.

Row 8: K1, p1, k1, p4, k1, p1, k1.

Row 9: [K1, p1] twice, m1, k2, m1, [p1, k1] twice–12 sts.

Row 10: [K1, p1] 3 times, [p1, k1] 3 times.

Row 11: Work 5 sts in Seed st as established, pm, m1, k2, m1, pm, work in Seed st as established to end–14 sts.

Rows 12, 14, 16, 18, and 20: Work in Seed st to first marker, knit the knit sts and purl the purl sts to next marker, work in Seed st to end.

Row 13: Work to first marker, k1, m1, work to 1 st before next marker, m1, k1, work to end–16 sts.

Rows 15, 17, and 19: Work to first marker, k1, m1-p, work to 1 st before next marker, m1-p, k1, work to end–22 sts after Row 19.

Row 21: Work to first marker, k1, m1-p, pm, work across Chart C to 1 st before next marker, pm, m1-p, k1, work to end–24 sts.

Rows 22, 24, 26, 28, 30, 32, 34, and 36: Work even as established.

Rows 23, 25, 27, 29, 31, and 33: Work to first marker, k1, m1-p, work to 1 st before fourth marker, m1-p, k1, work to end–36 sts after Row 33.

Row 35: P2tog, work to first marker, k1, m1-p, work to 1 st before fourth marker, m1-p, k1, work to last 2 sts, p2tog.

Row 37: K2tog, work to first marker, k1, m1-p, work to 1 st before fourth marker, removing second and third markers, m1-p, k1, work to last 2 sts, k2tog.

Row 38: Work to first marker, p1, pm for new beginning of Chart, work to 1 st before next marker, pm for new end of Chart, p1, work to end.

Row 39: Work to first marker, sm, k1, m1-p, sm, work to 1 st before fourth marker, sm, m1-p, k1, sm, work to end–38 sts. Work even until Rows 18-61 of Chart C have been worked 4 times. Work Rows 18-54 of Chart C once, removing second and third markers on last row (piece should measure approximately 42" along the edge [46" from bottom of point]).

SHAPE PIECE

Row 1: K1-f/b, work to first marker, k1, p2tog, p8, pm, work across Row 1 of Chart C, pm, purl to 3 sts before next marker, p2tog, k1, work to last st, k1-f/b.

Row 2 and all WS Rows: Work even as established, removing second and third markers on Row 18.

Row 3: P1-f/b, work to first marker, k1, p2tog, work to 3 sts before fourth marker, p2tog, k1, work to last st, p1-f/b.

Rows 5, 7, 9, 11, 13, 15, 17, 19, and 21: Work to first marker, k1, p2tog, work to 3 sts before fourth marker, p2tog, k1, work to end–20 sts remain after Row 21. *Note: Stop working Chart after completing Row 17.*

Row 23: Work to first marker, k1, p2tog, m1-p, ssk, k2tog, m1-p, p2tog, k1, work to end–18 sts remain.

Row 25: Work to first marker, k1, p2tog, k2, p2tog, k1, work to end–16 sts remain.

Row 27: Work to first marker, remove marker, ssk, k2, k2tog, remove marker, work to end–14 sts remain.

Row 29: [K1, p1] twice, ssk, k2, k2tog, work to end–12 sts remain.

Row 31: K1, p1, k1, p2tog, k2, p2tog, work to end–10 sts remain.

Row 33: K1, p1, ssk, k2, k2tog, work to end–8 sts remain.

Row 35: K1, p2tog, k2, p2tog, k1–6 sts remain.

Row 37: Ssk, k2, k2tog–4 sts remain.

Row 39: Ssk, k2tog–2 sts remain. BO all sts.

Piece D–Intermediate

Work as for Piece B through Row 22.

Row 23: Work to first marker, k1, p2, m1-p, k1, work to end–13 sts.

Row 24 and all WS Rows: Work to first marker, knit the knit sts and purl the purl sts to next marker, work to end.

Rows 25 and 27: Work to 1 st before second marker, m1, k1, work to end–15 sts after Row 27.

Row 29: Work to first marker, k1, p3, k2, m1-p, k1, work to end–16 sts.

Row 31: Work to first marker, work across first 7 sts of Chart D, work to 1 st before next marker, m1-p, k1, work to end–17 sts. *Note: On following rows, continue to work Chart D, working 1 additional st from chart before each increased st. Work cable sts in St st until enough sts are available to work a complete cable.*

CHART A

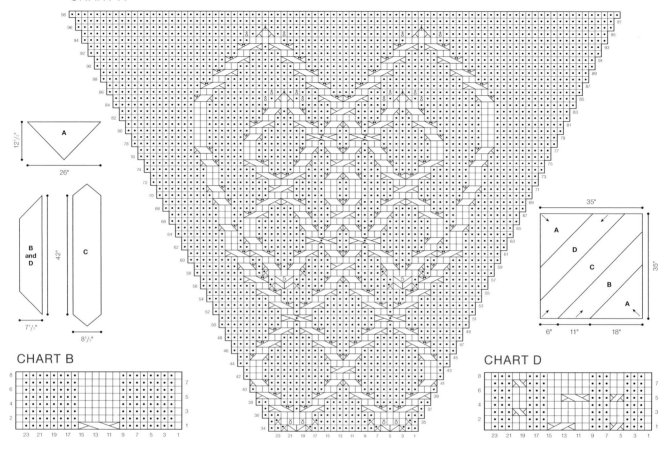

CHART B

CHART D

Rows 33, 47, 49, 51, and 57: Work to 1 st before second marker, m1-p, k1, work to end–30 sts after Row 57.

Rows 35, 37, 39, 41, 43, 45, 53, and 55: Work to 1 st before second marker, m1, k1, work to end–29 sts after Row 55.

Row 59: Work to 1 st before second marker, m1-p, k1, work to last 2 sts, p2tog.

Row 61: Work to 1 st before second marker, m1-p, k1, work to last 2 sts, k2tog. Place removable marker at end of row. Work even until piece measures 26" from removable marker, ending with a WS row.

SHAPE PIECE

Row 1: Work to 3 sts before second marker, p2tog, k1, work

to last st, k1-f/b.

Row 2 and all WS Rows: Work even as established.

Row 3: Work to 3 sts before second marker, p2tog, k1, work to last st, p1-f/b.

Row 5 and all RS Rows through Row 43: Work to 3 sts before second marker, work 2 sts together (p2tog if the next st to be worked is a purl st; k2tog if the next st to be worked is a knit st), work to end–10 sts remain after Row 43.

Row 45: K1, p1, k1, k2tog, work to end–9 sts remain.

Row 47: K1, p1, k2tog, work to end–8 sts remain.

Row 49: K1, p1, k2tog, work to end–7 sts remain.

Rows 51 and 55: Work to last 2 sts, p2tog–4 sts remain after

KEY

☐ Knit on RS, purl on WS.

• Purl on RS, knit on WS.

⅊ Make 1 knitwise.

⅄ Make 1 purlwise.

◹ P1-f/b, then pick up vertical strand running beneath st just made and p1 into strand.

◹5 K1, m1, k1, m1, k1.

◿ K2tog on RS.

◺ Ssk on RS.

⊠ P2tog on RS, k2tog on WS.

⊠ P2tog-tbl on RS, k2tog-tbl on WS.

⋏ Slip next 2 sts to right-hand needle as if to k2tog, pass first st over second st. Slip st purlwise back to left-hand needle, pass second st on left-hand needle over first st, k1–2 sts decreased.

◿ Knit into front of second st, then knit into first st, slip both sts from left-hand needle together.

◺ Knit into back of second st, then knit into front of first st, slip both sts from left-hand needle together.

◿ Slip next st to cn, hold to back, k2, p1 from cn.

◺ Slip 2 sts to cn, hold to front, p1, k2 from cn.

◿ Slip 2 sts to cn, hold to back, k2, k2 from cn.

◺ Slip 2 sts to cn, hold to front, k2, k2 from cn.

◿ Slip 2 sts to cn, hold to back, k2, p2 from cn.

◺ Slip 2 sts to cn, hold to front, p2, k2 from cn.

◿ Slip next 3 sts to cn, hold to back, k2, slip last st from cn to left-hand needle, p1, k2 from cn.

◺ Slip next 3 sts to cn, hold to front, k2, slip last st from cn to left-hand needle, p1, k2 from cn.

◺ Slip next 3 sts to cn, hold to front, k3, k3 from cn.

Row 55.

Rows 53 and 57: Work to last 2 sts, k2tog–3 sts remain after Row 57.

Row 59: Work to last 2 sts, p2tog–2 sts remain. BO all sts.

FINISHING

Block all five pieces to measurements at same time. Sew edges together (see Diagram). **Braided Bows:** Cut 12 strands of yarn 2 yards long; slip strands through center st at one corner of Blanket, secure with a knot. Work Overhand Braid (see page 156). Repeat in same corner for second Braid. Tie Braids into bow. Repeat for remaining corners.

CHART C

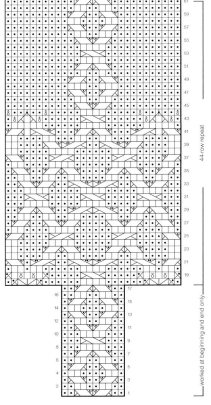

Chapter Five Giving

Making something for another person is a profound act. In a world where we often become obsessed with "quick gifts" and piling up FOs (finished objects), it's too easy to forget what a fundamental and meaningful gesture it is to knit something and give it away.

Giving is at the very heart of the knitting experience and the culture of knitting together. Some of the earliest organized knitalongs were intended to create gifts in times of need or celebration. Today many knitalong gifts are given out of love, out of charity, to bring hope to a hopeless situation, or literally to warm someone cold. Knitting can be a pure expression of support and joy, or a way to help someone suffering when nothing seems quite sufficient.

Not that there aren't selfish aspects to this, of course. There is a pleasure to the knitting, using yarns and patterns you might not otherwise try. There's a pleasure to the giving. If you're lucky, you may see someone's eyes light up when they open a hand-knitted gift. From the magical unfolding of an heirloom baby blanket, to the resonance and fortitude you feel when contributing warm hats to disaster relief, to the straight-out pleasure of seeing a friend wear every day that scarf you made, giving away your knitting can give you the pleasure of touching other people with your work.

There aren't any guarantees, of course. Knitters are perhaps the most hopeful of gift givers (or perhaps are just daft) as they spend hours and hours on gifts knowing full well the recipients may not really like them or appreciate the work that went into them.

Likewise, knitters must occasionally recognize that knitting may not always be the only answer to human needs. In the case of tragedy, sometimes the best thing to give is money, which can make a direct difference

without the wait for a warm garment to make its way off your needles. After the Indian Ocean tsunami disaster of December 2004, Stephanie Pearl-McPhee started Tricoteuses Sans Frontières, or Knitters Without Borders—an online fund-raiser through which knitters have donated more than $300,000 to support Médecins Sans Frontières (Doctors Without Borders). On the fund-raiser's web page, Stephanie challenges knitters to give their yarn money to the cause for one week: "Be honest," she writes. "Yarn is not (sob) necessary . . . Search yourself and ask, do I need this, or would the money be better spent on someone whose life hangs in the balance?" Other knitter-coordinated fund-raising efforts include Cara Davis's Spin Out, a spinning event in Manhattan that raised nearly $19,000 for Heifer International in 2006.

Yet sometimes knitting truly is part of the solution. There are times when a hat can save a life in winter, or a blanket can mend a broken heart. In these times, knitters shouldn't underestimate the power of their creations. The key, say charity organizers, is to use high-quality materials and make sure your item fits the needs of the organization or person receiving it.

In this chapter, we look at three ways knitters exercise their generosity with each other and the world, and we match those stories with projects that are just right for giving. First, we look at gifts for those most sympathetic recipients—other knitters!—with a story about the whirling microcosm of knitterly swapalongs. The Knitter's Magic Yarn Ball is a gift destined to be adored by fellow crafters. In contrast, anyone can appreciate the Traveling Scarf: a gift that travels from knitter to knitter, being built up along the way, until it reaches its final destination, the recipient. It's a perfect gift for a group to give a friend leaving on a journey—whether it's to a new land, a new job, or simply a new state of mind.

Next, we look beyond our circles of crafters and friends to the whole circle of life. Knitters are starting to connect their passion for fiber to the environment and animal rights. We suggest several ways knitters can reduce the impact of their crafty activities on the earth. One of the best and easiest ways is using recycled yarn or the knitted fabric in cast-off garments in place of new material—a concept we tried out with our own recycle-along and gallery. The results are delightful and inspiring. If you need a push getting started, give our Recycled Sweater Pincushion a spin.

Finally we invite you to knit for people in need—whether it is with a formal charity project, a good cause tinged with political activism, or simply a gift for somebody who really needs a show of support. As we survey the ways knitters have come together to help their fellow humans—from the Dulaan Project's warm hats for children to a marvelous knitted river made to promote clean water—we focus on the humble knitted square. Squares are the essential building blocks of thousands of community projects around the world: small enough to knit in a timely fashion, and standard enough to assemble into blankets that warm the body and spirit.

We ran our own square-along to make knitted quilts for charity and discovered something magical as we sewed up the contributions. The disparate squares, so jostled and mismatched in the box, started merging into a vibrant patchwork, a little symphony of kindness. The Barn-Raising Quilt was a knitalong of spirit as well as yarn. We hope you'll build one of your own.

Swaps and Giving to Friends

Ramona's Cupcake. St. Cloud. Shady Plum Grove. Knitters everywhere were thrilling to the clunk of the mailbox as 280 skeins of hand-dyed yarn with these intriguing color names arrived in the post. These colorful skeins were being shipped around the globe thanks to an online swap called Dye-O-Rama. In this "swapalong," each participant pledged to send a single skein of hand-dyed sock yarn to an assigned partner.

The majority of the participants had never dyed yarn before, according to Scout, a.k.a. Jamie Dixon, fiber artist and founder of the Dye-O-Rama swap. This led to hundreds of dyeing adventure posts around the blogosphere. It was pure fun. "People complained it was over too soon!" she enthuses.

For generations, there have been swap meets, where people bring their extra yarn to a central location—someone's house, a café, a school lunchroom—and exchange stashes with one another. In a twist on that concept, online versions proliferate today. And the Dye-O-Rama swap is just one example.

Sometimes online swaps are direct knitter-to-knitter trades that are coordinated by exchanging e-mails or posting on bulletin boards or photo-sharing sites. Other times, they are international round-robin affairs—the knitter's version of a pen-pal program. Participants are matched with one another either by the swap host or by a web-bot, a software program that does the work of matching and doling out addresses. Often, people are given questionnaires about their preferences to make the gifting more fun for both giver and receiver. Some people answer the questionnaires on their blogs, letting the whole world share in their thoughts about color and fiber preferences.

Online round-robin swaps are often coordinated by one volunteer blogger, but larger swaps may be handled by a whole team, as was the case with Dye-O-Rama. "There was no way I could have done this myself," says Scout. She was expecting a few dozen sign-ups, maybe seventy. When she saw the number of sign-ups rising past 100, then 200, then 250, she quickly recruited two co-organizers and an infinitely helpful husband of a friend (he wrote computer programs that handled swap pal match-ups and allowed the hosts to monitor swap activity). "Each host had our own group of about seventy-five people for which we were responsible," says Scout. "We answered our group's questions and made sure they got their packages out in time and that everyone received one."

Like Dye-O-Rama, other online knitting swaps are based on trading one's own handiwork. An example is the wildly popular Sockapalooza swap invented and hosted by Alison Hansel of The Blue Blog. Started in 2005, Sockapalooza invited swappers to exchange completed pairs of hand-knit socks made to specifications provided by swapees. The socks made by these secret knitting pals have gotten more and more elaborate with each term of the swap (Sockapaltwoza, Sockapaloooza, and Sockapalooza Four have all been successful follow-ups to the first go-round). Since the first swap, more than 2,000 pairs of socks have been knitted and mailed around the world, from Brussels to Boise.

Besides swapping finished objects, knitters often organize swaps for materials. A swap might be based on a particular kind of yarn, such as a sock yarn swap or a springtime cotton swap. Others are based on color, such as the Project Spectrum swaps that began sweeping the Internet in 2006. A craft-along celebrating the color wheel, Project Spectrum was created by a blogger from Washington, D.C., known as LollyKnitting Around. Every two months a set of colors is chosen and hundreds of crafters and bloggers around the world explore those colors with a variety of media: knitting projects, art, photography, and other crafts, writing, blogging, cooking, and more. Color-themed swaps—of everything from postcards to, of course, yarn—have sprung up around Project Spectrum, adding to the fun.

With any of these online swaps, sometimes you know who your partners are, and sometimes you don't. Keeping it secret is half the fun. The popularity of the international Secret Pal swaps proves it. Early in 2004, a blogger named Sandy of Sandy's Knitting started pairing knitters around the world in a Secret-Santa-like arrangement. Each participant was assigned a person to give gifts to and a dollar guideline to follow, but otherwise had free rein to spoil their pal. And spoil they did. People went wild, sometimes mailing far more than the called-for amount of goodies. A typical package might include a hand-knit washcloth wrapped around French milled soap, a knitting tool case filled with chocolates, a Clover yarn-cutter pendant, three skeins of alpaca yarn, and a pattern to use it with. Another might be filled with knitting magazines, homemade cookies, a beautiful letterpress card, a gaggle of cotton yarn balls, and even a hand-knit hat.

In fact, for most swaps, part of the game is to enhance your package—whether its main content is a pair of socks or a hand-dyed skein of yarn—with additional gifts such as Altoid tins full of Chibi yarn needles, beaded stitch markers, delicious chocolate, coffee, or tea, and lovely wrapping tissue in brilliant colors. "In swap world, everyone is like that person at the office who exceeds the Secret Santa dollar limit," says Jeanmarie, a swapper from Sterling Heights, New Jersey.

Often, gifters will include trinkets and treats that are specific to where they live, sending something unique that the giftee would be unlikely to experience otherwise. A knitter from England might send a plum pudding and Bernat knitting needles to a knitter in Brooklyn, New York, who might in turn send classic New York black-and-white cookies along with her handspun yarn to a knitter in Florida.

"It's just so much fun to spoil someone," admits Jeanmarie. "It's also a thrill to get packages from faraway places. When you don't know who your Secret Pal is, and a package arrives stamped Royal Mail, it's exciting!" It's equally fun to see your items arrive when the recipient blogs about them. This part of the exchange is so important that a swap is considered virtually incomplete until the recipients write about what they receive, with pictures and written shrieks of delight. When a swap is in full swing, the blogs of participants are rife with pictures of baroque piles of yarn and gifts (which you can often find through a list of links at the host's blog).

It's important for knitters to remember to enjoy the experience for what it is—a lark. Not all swap partners are created equal. Some sign up and later find that they can't get their packages out on time. Thus, the concept of "angels" has developed among swap organizers. These are volunteers who are willing to send an extra package to someone whose partner has flaked out.

"The swap organizer has a lot of responsibility throughout the swap," Scout explains, "making sure people are contacting their partners, working on their swap projects, and most importantly, making sure everyone gets their packages. As with everything in life, there's always some dirty work."

But compared with the joy of watching all those skeins of gorgeous yarn appear on blogs, the dirty work seems to fade into distant memory, and Scout seems ready to do it all again.

She was especially happy to see people new to dyeing trying it for the first time as part of her swap. She had two groups of swappers—old pros and total beginners—and she estimates that 75 percent of the participants placed themselves in the second category. By creating Dye-O-Rama, she was able to share her passion for dyeing yarn with hundreds of people who had never tried it before.

Swapping is exactly that—an opportunity to share something you love while finding out about new things from those who swap with you. "The idea for Dye-O-Rama came out of my pure joy and excitement in learning how to hand-dye yarn," Scout says. "I taught myself after reading a few books and searching online, and I knew that others could learn this skill just as easily."

And so they did.

A Knitter's Magic Yarn Ball

Imagine knitting from a ball of yarn, and every so often finding a trinket or tiny tool as you unwind—a stitch marker, a bit of ribbon, or a set of new buttons. At the heart of this ball, you find a small round pincushion, an intriguing vintage row counter, or a ball of translucent handmade soap. The Knitter's Magic Yarn Ball is a gift that delivers this experience to a crafter whom you want to surprise and delight. It's a perfect project for a knitterly swap among two dear friends or 200 online acquaintances. (Inspired by a project in the book *The Children's Year,* Hawthorn Press.)

Traveling Scarf

Worked in a delicious assortment of hand-painted Koigu yarn that blends together beautifully, this scarf is designed to travel from knitter to knitter until it reaches the friend for whom it is intended. To personalize, each knitter can attach to his or her section a card or other little gift. The finished scarf is a collage of friendship the recipient can hold close whenever they need it.

FINISHED MEASUREMENTS 5" wide x approximately 9' long

YARN Koigu Painter's Palette Premium Merino (KPPPM) (100% merino wool; 175 yards / 50 grams): 1 hank each #P521 Gold/Green mix, #1305 Dark Brown, #2395 Mocha, #P509 Light Green, #P324 Green/Brown Mix, #P319 Khaki/Orchid Mix, #P621 Pink Mix, #P338 Orange

NEEDLES One pair straight needles size US 7 (4.5 mm)

NOTIONS Stitch holder (you may use scrap yarn in contrasting color)

GAUGE Not essential for this project. However, it is important that each knitter try to match the gauge of the previous knitter so that the different sections remain consistent with one another.

NOTES
This Scarf is designed to be worked by eight different knitters. The entire Scarf is worked using 2 strands of yarn held together.

SCARF
Knitter 1
With color of your choice, CO 44 sts.

BEGIN PATTERN
All Rows: Slip 1 st knitwise, k1, p2, *k2, p2; repeat from * to end. Work even until 10 yards of yarn remain, or until you have reached the desired length for your section. DO NOT

BO sts, and DO NOT cut yarn. Place all sts on stitch holder or waste yarn. Attach notes or gifts, if desired, on your scarf section, then pass along to Knitter 2.

Knitters 2-7
Transfer sts to needles. With 1 strand of yarn from previous section and 1 strand of color of your choice held together, work even as established for 10 rows. Drop strand from previous section and join second strand of your color; work even until only 10 yards of yarn remain or until you have reached the desired length for your section. Complete as for first section and pass along to next knitter.

Final Knitter
Work as for previous knitters until you have used nearly all your yarn or have reached the desired Scarf length. BO all sts loosely in pattern.

FINISHING (Completed by Final Knitter)
Weave in all ends and block lightly. Coordinate with your knitting group to give the gift together.

Giving to the Earth

She probably didn't look like a tree hugger.

It was the summer of 2006, and this mystery knitter—whose name and identity have been lost in the shifting streams and eddies of Internet archives—was flipping through the racks in a Malaysian thrift shop. Buried in the drifts of monster truck T-shirts and other ephemera of the global textile trade, she found it: thrift-shop gold. It was a pullover made of attractive white yarn, hardly used and without heavy machine-serged seams. It was just right for unraveling and converting to something new, a decidedly green way to acquire yarn.

At home she worked through the process of unraveling—"tedious but economical," she wrote, as the pullover had cost only 15 Malaysian *ringgit*, or about $4 –and started knitting with her harvest. The result showed she was no novice. The yarn became a sleeveless feather-weight top made entirely of diamond-paneled lace, with an intriguing square neckline. It looked entirely new; there was nothing secondhand about it.

She posted a picture and a few words to the blog Wardrobe Refashion, and disappeared back into anonymity—but not without gaining a few fans in the comments area first.

"WOW!"

"No one would believe it only cost $4."

"Did you use a pattern? Or design the top yourself? I love it."

These readers were a particularly appreciative audience, all being self-proclaimed "Refashionistas": crafters who have signed a public "contract" to abstain from the purchase of new manufactured items of clothing for two, four, or six months—however long they can last. (Certain items, like shoes and underwear, are excepted.) Instead, they swear to make what they want and need by refashioning, renovating, and recycling "preloved" items. Refashionistas from Japan, the United Kingdom, the United States, Australia, and other places gather virtually at the Wardrobe Refashion web space to encourage each other and show off their progress in knitting, sewing, and every other relevant craft.

Some do it to save money, some to protest sweatshop labor, some just for fun and a crafting challenge. But a growing motivation is the environment. Nichola Prested, a mom from Melbourne, Australia, gave birth to two baby girls and started thinking about the world they would inherit—and got inspired to start Wardrobe Refashion. "I want to be a good example for them," she says.

So what is the environmental effect of a yarn-buying habit? Most knitters may be relieved to know that their fiber addiction probably adds very little to their total impact on the planet.

According to a comprehensive study by the Union of Concerned Scientists and published partly in *The Consumers Guide to Effective Environmental Choices*, all personal items and services (clothing, entertainment, jewelry, and so on) only represent about 6 percent of the average American's contribution to greenhouse gas emissions, and 12 percent of their contribution to toxic water pollution. For most knitters, yarn purchases represent only a tiny fraction of those numbers. In contrast, transportation and household operations (heating, cooling, and so forth) represent more than 65 percent of contributions to greenhouse gasses and 37 percent of toxic water pollution.

If a knitter really wants to make a difference for the environment, housing and transportation are the best places to start. (Naturally, warm, cozy knitted socks, hats, and blankets can keep you warm while you turn down the thermostat and work on insulating your house.)

Nonetheless there's no reason knitters can't make their fiber life square perfectly with their environmental ideals. Every kind of yarn comes, at least potentially, with environmental baggage. Synthetic yarns draw very slightly on the unsustainable global oil supply. Cotton is a plant product with a reputation for being one of the most environmentally costly forms of agriculture, in terms of fertilizer, pesticides, and the overuse of irrigation. Wool is an animal product, sheared from sheep that graze on pasture and rangeland—and in the past have often overgrazed, with considerable consequences to the landscape.

One simple way to address concerns for cotton and wool is to buy certified organic products. To be certified, those yarns must be made with plants, rangeland, and animals that are free of chemical fertilizers or pesticides; overgrazing and excessive use of water are discouraged. But no matter what kind of yarn you use—animal, vegetable, or completely synthetic—there are potential environmental effects associated with dyeing and processing that yarn, and transporting it to you. To reduce those effects you might want to patronize local producers, or ones that utilize technologies that appeal to you, like natural dyes.

Unraveling and recycling yarn that's already been used is probably the smartest ecological choice of all. With a recycled project, there are no effects from the production or dyeing of new yarn, so you've brought the environmental impact of your yarn purchase down to nearly zero (especially if you walk or ride your bike to the thrift store).

"Yarn farming," as Pittsburgh mom Steph dubs it, isn't always easy. Before you get your harvest of beautiful cheap yarn, you need a "field" to work in—a source of cheap knitted items. Most people use a thrift store (some even sell sweaters by the pound), but there's always Mom's closet and, perhaps most emotionally challenging, your own trove of finished but less-than-loved projects.

Next, you need to choose your crops carefully. The thrift store will have a mix of hand- and machine-knitted sweaters with various construction methods.

"The key is to concentrate on quality," says Kristina from Washington State, author of a web tutorial on yarn recycling. First off, avoid sweaters with serged seams—usually visible as lots of overstitching with sewing thread along the inner seams. Unraveling these serged sweaters will typically yield large numbers of short pieces of yarn. Sweaters knit in the round or with seams like those used in hand-knits should provide more continuous yardage.

Next, Kristina says, look for yarn that you really want to work with, just as you would when purchasing new fiber. She prefers nonscratchy yarn, with a color that provides some potential for dyeing. She minimizes the need for heavy cleaning of the wool by looking for sweaters that have hardly been worn or washed.

After this comes unraveling, and the experience will vary with the sweater's construction. But don't be surprised if it's a challenge to find a starting point and to draw the yarn out into balls. It can be hard, messy work.

If reusing yarn sounds great, but this process doesn't, there's another way to recycle an old hand-knit or thrifted sweater almost magically. As long as it is wool, you can felt it and use the resulting fabric as the basis for projects ranging from arm warmers to bags to stuffed animals. Firmly felted fabric is especially easy to work with because you can cut its edges and they will not fray. (The easiest recycled sweater project ever is to felt a large sweater, then whack off the arms at the elbow—instant arm warmers!)

Either way—harvesting or felting—the trouble of recycling could have both a positive psychic and environmental impact. When you rework something, you're making a connection with the person who made it and touched it before—maybe another hand-knitter, maybe even yourself as you existed several years ago. An Aran sweater made by Grandma and accidentally felted in the wash can be given new life as the centerpiece to a blanket, and working with it can connect you to your ancestor in a knitalong-through-time. A mysterious child's jumper found in a thrift bin can make you muse about who might have made it, and share a moment of crafting with an unknown knitalonger.

"I found a sweater at a secondhand store that I don't wear a lot but have affection for," says knit blogger Bethany. "It's obviously a first sweater. Buttonholes don't match buttons. I think about the person who finished the sweater even with its imperfections. I wonder if they wonder where that sweater is now."

"I'm a bit of a nut about using things that have history," says another blogger, Ms. Knitingale. "I like to think about how things started their lives and who might've used them before. When you knit a garment, you put more into it than just the wool. Every inch of that fiber passes through the hands of the person who dreamed of the final garment. Pretty amazing when you think of it that way, no?"

Refashioning, Reknitting, Recycling

For more information,
check out these resources:

....

www.nikkishell.typepad.com/wardroberefashion/
The Wardrobe Refashion craft-along website.

The Consumer's Guide to Effective Environmental Choices: Practical Advice from the Union of Concerned Scientists
by Michael Brower (Three Rivers Press, 1999)
A good resource for getting beyond "paper vs. plastic" to make smarter environmental choices.

www.neauveau.com/recycledyarn.html
and www.az.com/~andrade/knit/thrifty.html
Tutorials on yarn recycling.

www.flintknits.blogspot.com/2007/04/
make-this-jacket_17.html
A tutorial by Pamela Wynne on how to make a stunning bike rider-style zippered jacket out of a way-too-big sweater.

www.craftster.org
A forum for sharing craft ideas and experiences, including many tutorials on felting sweaters and using the felted fabric to make all kinds of craft items.

When I look at knitting, I think about people. Even a sorry old machine-knit wool sweater has probably been touched by a dozen people on several continents on its journey from sheep's back to finished item on a store shelf to thrift bin at Goodwill. It's got a history that makes one hesitate to throw it out. (And often some awesome stripes to boot.)

All this history lends a special air to crafting from scrap or discarded materials—things that have been worn out or fallen hopelessly out of style. Recycled crafts are a way of making something new, while touching and honoring the work of all the hands that have gone before us. Recycling knits is also a great way to acknowledge the environmental impact of crafting (see page 134).

Martin and I wanted to promote both the artistic value of old knits-with-history, and the environmental value of crafting with recycled materials, so we ran a knitalong devoted to it, and called it a recycle-along.

Since there are so many ways of using recycled knitting materials, I didn't give out a pattern for this knitalong. Rather, I invited people to riff on the theme. I simply set up a page on an online photo-sharing site and asked people to send in pictures of something they had made using reclaimed yarn or recycled knitted fabric, explaining it well so others could appreciate their project.

Though it was simple, this knitalong was bursting with "out of the box" ideas. A few intrepid knitters ripped out whole sweaters to harvest the yarn, then re-knit something much more to their liking. Others used scrap knitting from old abandoned UFOs (unfinished objects) or used thrifted sweaters as cloth. Martin and I were amazed by the number of attractive and inventive uses people found for old knitting. Indeed, our recycle-along suggested that thrift-store sweaters are a major national resource!

It turned out that the knitalong format was a perfect one for sharing recycling ideas. The recycle-along was flexible enough so that a lot of people could join and have fun. And the array of goods made me—and prob-

ably a few other people, too—want to get out my sewing machine and start whacking up old sweaters and sewing them back together in new and different forms.

Most commonly, crafters took machine-knit sweaters that were knit in a finer gauge than most people would attempt by hand—such as those from chain fashion stores—and felted them in the washer and dryer. The resulting fuzzy, stretchy cloth could be cut and sewn into a cornucopia of lovely products. With a few cuts made and seams sewn, an old ski sweater could be transformed into a colorful hat or two, and the sleeves might become a Christmas stocking or cozy little pants for a child. Knitter Pamela Wynne made a gorgeous biker-style jacket out of a too-large, felted-down sweater to which she added knit-on cuffs and a collar. Other knitters felted down the fronts and the backs of cabled, Fair Isle, or plain Stockinette-stitch sweaters, reclaiming cloth fragments big enough to sew into tote bags, pillows, and crazy-quilt-like blankets—or even, in Martin's favorite project, a lovely stuffed elephant named Bakul.

Clearly, creativity does not require virgin materials. In fact, starting with used materials gives the crafter some structure within which to exercise creativity—always a winning setup.

And it lends some built-in history and character to a new project. The complete gallery at knitalong.net is the living proof.

There's nothing wrong with showing the provenance of the raw materials in our finished work, like using aged bricks or faded window frames from an old building in a new one. A bit of recycled spirit survives in Bakul's colorful trunk and body—a much finer end for a garment than simply being thrown away. I hope that when "the time comes" for things I have made, they'll be treated with as much kindness and consideration.

1. Michelle Russell, Santa Cruz, CA 2. Katy Murphy, Mesa, AZ
3. Alicia Paulson, Portland, OR 4. Pamela Wynne, Flint, MI
5. Heidi Butler, Kalamazoo, MI 6. Max Daniels, Boston, MA
7. Heidi Butler, Kalamazoo, MI 8. Larissa Brown, Portland, OR
9. Emily Simnitt, Boise, ID 10. Emily Simnitt, Boise, ID

Recycled Sweater Pincushion

You don't always need to unravel a sweater in order to recycle it. Run a wool sweater—a personal handknit gone wrong or a cardigan unearthed at your favorite thrift shop—through a hot, soapy wash and hot dryer. You'll end up with a dense, felted fabric that makes an intriguing material for these darling, near-to-bursting pincushions. DESIGN BY MESHELL TAYLOR

FINISHED MEASUREMENTS

Cubular Pincushion (see left): Approximately 3" high x 3" wide x 3" deep

Squashed Pincushion (see page 142): Approximately 1" high x 3" wide x 3" deep

MATERIALS Wool or wool blend sweater(s); rotary cutter, cutting mat and quilt ruler; polyester or wool stuffing; sewing machine and matching machine thread (optional); sewing needle and matching thread; long doll needle; six-stranded embroidery floss for binding; $5/8$" to 1" buttons (6 for Cubular, 2 for Squashed Cube); $3/4$" square scraps thick fabric with tight weave, or leftover felted scraps (6 for Cubular, 2 for Squashed Cube); embellishments (optional)

NOTES You can create either a Squashed Cube or a Cubular Pincushion. Both are made in a very similar fashion, though the Cubular Pincushion is twice the height of the Squashed Cube, and requires a few additional steps in the binding stage. The Cubular Pincushion is made up of 6 equal-sized pieces; the Squashed Cube Pincushion is made up of a square top and bottom, and 4 rectangular sides.

PINCUSHION

Felting

Felt the sweater(s) in a hot wash and hot dryer, keeping in mind that a very thick felted fabric may be harder to sew under the machine, but it will stay neat when bound; thinner, more open weave felted fabric may be easier to shape and sew but harder to control when binding. Experiment and play around with your materials!

Cutting

Using rotary cutter and quilt ruler, cut pieces from the felt as follows: Pressing firmly on the ruler to keep the fabric from stretching or moving, cut six $3^1/2$" squares for the Cubular Pincushion, and two $3^1/2$" squares and four $1^1/2$" x $3^1/2$" rectangles for the Squashed Cube Pincushion.

Sewing

Designate one square as your base, and with RS's of pieces together, sew two opposite sides to the base. Use a machine st length of about $2^1/2$ mm and a $1/4$" seam. Leave $1/4$" unsewn at beginning and end of each seam (to ease and neaten turning inside-out later). Secure all lines of stitching with back stitching at each end.

Sew on the two remaining sides in the same manner. Then sew on the top, attaching it to all sides, and leaving a small hole in one of the corners, with back stitching before and after the hole. *Note: Once you've sewn up the side seams, you will push the finished Pincushion RS-out through this hole, then stuff the Pincushion through it.* Sew the side seams.

Turn the sewn Pincushion RS-out. Using a blunt-pointed object (a knitting needle is perfect!), poke out all the corners, being careful not to poke through the fabric or seams.

Stuffing

Stuff the Pincushion using very small pieces; it should look very fat when you are done. The square shapes will become defined when you start binding. Using sewing needle and matching thread, hand-sew the hole you left. Work the Pincushion with your hands to distribute stuffing evenly.

Binding

The first step of binding is to create an indentation in the center of each side. For the Cubular Pincushion, you will make 6 indentations; for the Squashed Cube Pincushion, you will make 2 (in the base and top).

Using embroidery floss and doll needle, thread a $^3/_4$" square of thick, tightly woven fabric onto knotted thread before you start (this will keep the knot from being pulled through the Pincushion). Insert the needle into the center of the first side, through the Pincushion and out the center of the opposite side. Sew back and forth through the center of both sides, keeping the thread tension tight, until you have created the desired depth of indent in the Pincushion, ending on the second side. Thread a second scrap of fabric onto the needle, pushing it flush with the Pincushion before tying a knot. Trim floss. Repeat for the remaining sides of the Cubular Pincushion.

Cut one long piece of embroidery floss and knot the end (36" long for Cubular Pincushion; 24" long for Squashed Pincushion). For the Cubular Pincushion, using the doll needle, pass the floss through the woven fabric at the center of the top of the Pincushion to secure the knot, bring the needle out through the center of an adjacent side (not the base); wrap the floss around the middle of the side and back down into the center of the top. Bring the needle through the center of the next adjacent side. Continue as established until all 6 sides have been wrapped (see photo, page 140). For the Squashed Cube Pincushion, work as for the Cubular Pincushion, working through the center of the top and base. Tie off and trim floss as above.

Adjust the binding if necessary to make sure it lies down the middle of each side and that the stuffing on all sides of the binding is even. Pinch all the outer corners of the Pincushion into shape.

Embellishment

Sew buttons on 2 at a time, working 1 each on opposite sides, sewing through each button at least twice to secure them. When finishing, bring floss out behind (not through) one of the buttons, split the strand in half and take the pieces around the threads that are holding the button in place. Knot the halves together 3 times; this will keep the knot from being pulled through the felted fabric. Trim floss.

If desired, thread beads onto pins and poke into place, or glue for more permanent decoration.

Giving to People in Need

"The best thing about my afghan, the thing that I love, is that each square has a meaning," says Lynn Siprelle, a knitter and spinner who received a hand-knit afghan after she suffered two heart attacks, and was revived from near-death. Her afghan was made of squares from friends the world over. They knew Lynn through her blog, her local knitting circle, and various online forums. They mailed their knitted squares to two local knitters, who coordinated the sewing up and bestowed the blanket on Lynn.

It was a "charity" knitalong in the best, most general, sense of the word—neighbors, friends, and strangers getting together to care for someone who needed help. Projects like this are going on all the time, whether they're called knitalongs or not. Often they're ad hoc collaborations, but sometimes for-mal organizations sponsor or grow up around the projects.

Knitting for Peace, a 2006 book by Betty Christian-sen, celebrated some of the most interesting and success-ful charity knitalongs. The Dulaan Project collects knitted items to warm Mongolian people for whom hand-knits can save lives during extreme winters. Project Linus has delivered just shy of two million new handmade blankets to children who have been traumatized, are seriously ill, or are otherwise in need. The Prayer Shawl Ministry com-bines spiritual practice, knitting, and compassion for oth-ers. Knitters, solo or in groups, work on shawls and imbue them with their prayers and well wishes, to donate in their own ways in their own communities.

A few efforts reach out to animals. In 2001, the Tas-manian Conservation Trust's Penguin Jumpers Project captured knitters' imaginations with a unique temporary project creating sweaters for penguins covered in oil from oil slicks. The "jumpers" arrived by the thousands, and helped keep penguins from grooming themselves and ingesting the toxic oil until they were well enough to be safely cleaned by humans.

So why does charity knitting fill up such a large corner of the knitalong universe?

"For knitters, it's great to be able to do something we love to do—knit—and have it be helpful," says Kay Gardiner, coauthor of *Mason-Dixon Knitting*. Kay and writing partner Ann Shayne organized a wildly popular knitalong to benefit a program called afghans for Afghans, which collects hand-knit blankets and clothing for people in Afghanistan. Kay feels that in a time of crisis, people want to be given "marching orders" and concrete ways they can help. Asking a knitter to make an afghan square achieves that perfectly. Ann and Kay's knitalong collected squares—more than 1,000, before they stopped counting—that could then be assembled into warm blankets (or "afghans"). The Warm Up America! Foundation has processed even more squares—*hundreds* of thousands—in one way or another. This organization, which might be the mothership for all charitable afghan squares, coordinates volunteers who create handmade blankets out of donated squares, and also encourages local knitting groups every-

where to make blankets and donate them directly within their own communities.

Efforts like these have extended the warmth of charitable blankets to victims of war, to the sick in hospital rooms everywhere, to the dispossessed and displaced in trailers and camps in the wake of natural disasters, and to people worldwide making a new start for a dozen other reasons.

Knitted squares just might ultimately represent all the things this book is about—pitching in, collaborating, inspiring and being inspired, and becoming part of something bigger than oneself. They are perhaps the most social little projects in any knitter's basket: meant to be given, and in the giving to create comfort, accomplishment, and fulfillment. Creating an afghan can be the knitting world's equivalent of a barn-raising.

The square's simplicity belies its power: to warm a cold lap, give comfort to a child, change a life. The Knit A River project from the international charity WaterAid aims to use squares to go even further and change the world. Working with London-based yarn shop I Knit, WaterAid is assembling a river-sized petition of blue knitted squares to publicize the need to bring clean water and effective sanitation to the world's neediest people.

Seen up close, the squares are personalized with messages and drawings; from far away the petition curves and ripples just like a real river. The project's watery-blue blog proclaims, "I Knit is proud to be making a spectacle! WATER AND TOILETS FOR ALL!" It seems few knitters can argue with that. The group has collected more than 40,000 squares.

But sometimes a world-changing assembly of squares comes softly, with less fanfare. It takes only a few warm squares to save a life, as heart attack survivor Lynn Siprelle knows.

She lists out her squares like a litany or prayer: "Anhata's square was knit with yarn that I'd watched her try to knit into a vest no less than five times before she gave up; it reminds me of all the laughing we did over that damned vest . . . Melisa's square was knit with yarn that I taught her to ply . . . Zillah's square came all the way from Britain, the same with Honey's. It made two faraway online friends real somehow."

Her favorite square is an "irregular but heartfelt" one contributed by one of her knitting circle members' sons, Jonah, who is eleven. "He could hardly contain himself until I noticed that square."

If anyone ever wonders whether they should take the time to knitalong on an afghan for someone in need, Lynn has the answer. "Sometimes I would wonder if I shouldn't have just stayed dead. But seeing and using my blankie reminded me there are people here who care about and need me," she says. "I nap under it almost every day. In fact, Melisa wanted it back so she could block it and I won't give it back. Block, schmock."

Knitting for Others

Here are some places to begin:

·····································

www.interweave.com/knit/charities.asp,
http://cache.lionbrand.com/
charityConnection.html,
www.woolworks.org/charity.html
Websites with contact information for dozens of charity knitting organizations.

www.warmupamerica.com
Warm Up America! Foundation's homepage, with links to tips on sewing up afghans and donating in your own community.

www.fireprojects.org/dulaan.htm
Website for the Dulaan Project.

www.projectlinus.org
Website for Project Linus.

www.wateraid.org/knitariver
Website for WaterAid's Knit a River project.

www.afghansforafghans.org
Website for afghans for Afghans.

www.shawlministry.com
Website for Prayer Shawl Ministry.

Knitting for Peace: Make the World a Better Place One Stitch at a Time by Betty Christiansen (Stewart, Tabori & Chang 2006) Book of stories, projects, and tips for charitable knitting.

 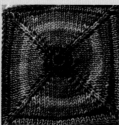   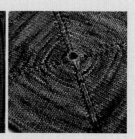

larissa's
BARN-RAISING
QUILT
Knitalong Diary

I smacked my forehead when I realized what the last knitalong for our book needed to be. Squares are so perfect for a joint knitting effort. They embody so many of the great things about knitalongs: the variety, repetition, range of color, the knitter's play within a structured pattern, and the generosity of spirit I experience every time I work with volunteer knitters. Squares were clearly the perfect subject for a knitalong to wrap up our chapter on giving, and this book.

An intriguing square virtually fell into my lap one day when I visited the blog Knitting Iris and followed a link to a pattern by Shelley Mackie. Shelley quickly agreed to be part of the book, and we were off.

I wrote a plea on my blog to recruit test knitters. Each would choose his or her own sock yarn to make a square. The squares would be mailed to me, and I'd assemble them into the Barn-Raising Quilt.

I didn't set a sign-up limit. I figured I'd use any extra squares to make blankets for charity. How many could that be? Well . . . thank goodness Martin figured out how to automate the sign-ups at knitalong.net, because by the end there were 500 knitters.

As squares started popping up on the Web and arriving in my mailbox, I wasn't quite prepared for the explosions and rivulets of color. They were vivid and fascinating. The focus on sock yarn had paid off! But a sneaking suspicion started tugging at me. What if all these amazing squares looked, well, awful together?

The colors tended to jostle and compete no matter how I laid them out, and with such a variety of yarns, the squares varied in size. Fortunately, exacting standards didn't seem crucial for this project. ("Wonkiness is a gift," I kept repeating to myself. It was something I'd read on the Mason-Dixon Knitting blog, and it seemed apropos to this group-knitted blanket.)

I stuck to my plan, and finally a color story began to emerge. Soon it seemed like the squares were literally made for one another, rather than made by people so far apart they would likely never meet.

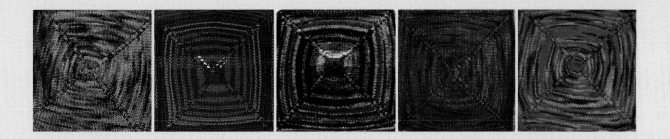

While I was sewing the blanket together, I had a bad moment where I thought I wouldn't finish in time. Martin encouraged me to think of one wonderful, dependable person I could ask for help. I instantly thought of JJ, a woman I barely knew but could tell was great, and whose knitting I admired. She dropped everything and met me at Mabel's Café for two days in a row, and we became friends over sewing and lattes. It was this book come to life.

It got me thinking tenderly about knitters. We have the desire to pitch in. We want to do good work. These are desires most knitters have shared for all time, from ancient sailors to the mothers of soldiers to anyone making a scarf for a friend. It's an impulse that seems especially strong when people are knitting *together*, whether they're winding balls of yarn in a kitchen or trading tips across ten thousand miles, connected only by the glassy threads of the Internet.

Making this blanket made me feel a bit like Dr. Seuss's Grinch, whose heart grows three sizes when he discovers the true spirit of Christmas. I remember holding the first squares in my hands and think-

ing, This is Siri's knitting, right here! She *made* this square! People I'd known only online had sent the work of their very hands to me. It was deeply moving. It reminded me to never forget—knitting is special. It's not quick. It's not funky. It's not easy-peasey. It's work, often hard work, loving work we do for one another.

With recent technology, it's become easier to do this knitting work together. I hope that means the knitters' spirit of pitching in, and of comfort through touch, can take root and spread easier, too. A blanket may not seem like much compared to the specters of disaster and heartbreak. But it might just be the thing to help someone look up again.

1. Beth Braun, Seattle, WA 2. Chawne Kimber, Easton, PA 3. JJ Heldmann, Portland, OR 4. S. Larsen, MT 5. Angela Tong, New York, NY 6. Kathy Yurman, Juneau, AK 7. S. Larsen, MT 8. Betsy Hart, Conway, AR 9. Valerie Wallis, Logan, UT 10. Karrie Weaver, Berkeley, CA

Barn-Raising Quilt

An afghan made by many knitters is the barn-raising of all knitting projects, the kind of effort where the more people pitch in, the warmer—and wilder—the results. DESIGN BY SHELLEY MACKIE, LARISSA BROWN, AND 36 KNITTERS FROM AROUND THE WORLD

FINISHED MEASUREMENTS Squares: $7^1/_2$" before sewing; 7" after sewing; Afghan: $42^1/_2$" wide x $49^1/_2$" long, after blocking

YARN

Squares: Approximately 3000 yards of fingering weight yarn (MC) that knits to gauge of 7 to $7^1/_2$ sts per inch, such as Lorna's Laces Shepherd Sock, Blue Moon Fiber Arts® Socks that Rock® lightweight, Koigu KPPPM, ShiBui Sock, Hello Yarn Hand-Dyed Sock, Regia 4-ply Sock Yarns, Opal Sock Yarns, and Skacel Trekking XXL; shown in broad range of sock yarns. *Note: 50-gram ball fingering weight yarn yields approximately 3 squares.*

Edging: Rowan Classic Yarns Cashsoft Aran (57% extra-fine merino / 33% microfiber / 10% cashmere; 95 yards / 50 grams): 1 ball #15 Sienna (A)

NEEDLES One set of five double-pointed needles (dpn) size US 2 (2.75 mm). Change needle size if necessary to obtain correct gauge.

NOTIONS Crochet hook size US G/6 (4 mm); stitch markers; removable marker; row counter

GAUGE 30 sts and 43 rows = 4" (10 cm) in Stockinette stitch (St st) within Square

QUILT

Square (make 42)

With MC and needle size of your choice, CO 12 sts, divide among 4 dpn. Join for working in rnd, being careful not to twist sts; place removable marker for beginning of rnd.

Rnd 1: Knit.
Rnd 2: *K1, yo, place marker (pm), k1, yo, k1; repeat from * around–20 sts.
Rnd 3: Knit.
Rnd 4: *Knit to marker, yo, slip marker (sm), k1, yo, knit to end of needle; repeat from * around.
Repeat Rnds 3 and 4 eighteen times–172 sts (43 sts each needle). Knit 1 rnd. BO all sts loosely. *Note: As Square grows, move beginning of rnd marker, as necessary.*

FINISHING

Block each Square to $7^1/_2$" square. Lay out 6 columns of 7 Squares each. Sew 6-Square columns first, then sew columns to one another using tapestry needle and waste yarn or tails from BO, as follows: Holding 2 Squares alongside one another, with RSs facing up, allow BO edges to curl upward against one another so WSs touch and form a decorative ridge. Working from RS, sew running stitch just under this ridge (in last row of knitting before BO). Sew st in every 2 or so BO sts, being careful not to pull tightly. Your sts will be hidden under BO ridge. Every 10 sts or so, work ridge with your fingers to even out tension.

Crochet Edging:

Rnd 1 (RS): With RS facing, using crochet hook and A, beginning 1 st up from one corner of Quilt, work single crochet (sc) sts around Quilt, working sc in approximately 2 out of every 3 edge sts, and working 3 scs in each corner st to turn corner; slip st to join beginning of rnd. Turn Quilt over.
Rnd 2 (WS): Loosely work slip st in each sc around Quilt; slip st to join beginning of rnd. Fasten off. Weave in all ends. Reblock Quilt.

Doing It Yourself

There are as many kinds of knitalongs as there are friends to knit with, each one a unique snowflake of an experience. We hope you've been inspired by this book and are thinking about starting one of your own. This chapter offers questions you might want to ask yourself before diving in and inviting your first friend to cast on with you.

WHY KNIT TOGETHER?

Every knitalong has a purpose, and thinking about why you want to start a knitalong project, knitting group, or meet-up can help guide you in its design. For some knitalongs, the purpose is as simple as ongoing companionship and fun. Other knitalongs are goal-oriented, with a finished gift, charity project, or art project in mind. Most fall somewhere between these two extremes, with a purpose that's part friendship and part collaboration, friendly competition, inspiration, learning, and giving.

WHAT IS YOUR KAL ABOUT?

Every knitalong has a theme. To identify yours, it may help to ask yourself what you would name your knitalong. Here are a few fictional examples: a KAL focused on a single pattern (the French Press Cozy-Along), a technique (Intarsia-Rama), a specific yarn (the Brown Sheep Roundup), a charitable project (Blankets for Bunnies), or an art project (the 10,000 Doilies Installation). If your purpose is getting together on a regular basis with a group of friends, your theme might simply be Potluck Tuesdays or Sip & Knit Night.

WILL YOU KNIT TOGETHER IN PERSON OR ONLINE?

Your knitalong may be online only, you may mix online sign-ups with in-person meetings at a local yarn shop, library, or public park, or you might recruit people on the Internet but have them send the knitted work to one location to be compiled. The combinations are endless.

If you're choosing a location to meet in person, consider important elements like seating, lighting, atmosphere, and noise level. If you're meeting in public, make sure it's a place everyone can find and easily reach, and where the proprietors don't mind a group that stays a while. If you're meeting at someone's home, consider rotating the hosting responsibilities or making each meeting a potluck.

If you opt for the Internet, make sure you give your KAL a strong online presence. This may include a Web address or blog of its own, or a clearly defined "home post" on your own blog, which other people can easily link to. It may also include a unique and consistent "look and feel." Consider going beyond the standard templates provided by the blogging software companies when you design your KAL homepage. Knitalongers appreciate links to their own websites listed on the KAL site. And most like to have a logo or "button" they can save and use to show their affiliation.

HOW WILL YOU GET PEOPLE TO JOIN?

A knitalong is only as fun as the knitters who join, and promoting your KAL—whether it be to a few friends or to the entire world—is part of your job as organizer. If you are looking to recruit local members for an in-person meet-up, ask the management at your LYS whether they can help you hook up with like-minded knitters. Also consider using electronic resources, such as Groups.yahoo.com (many cities and towns have dedicated "SnB" Yahoo groups already online, where you can advertise an in-person meet-up) and Craigslist.com. For online KALs, ask knit bloggers to help you spread the word. Also ask everyone who joins the KAL to blog about it and link to your KAL homepage. Consider using public forums—craft sites like Craftster.org and the knitting and crochet community at Ravelry.com, bulletin boards like Knittyboards.com, the discussion sections of groups on Flickr.com, and clearinghouse sites like Knitalongs.xaviermuskateer.com.

WHAT'S THE DURATION?

Most happy knitalongs have a duration that is announced right at the beginning, so knitters know what to expect. In some cases the duration is central to the knitalong's theme. For example, a quick search of past online knitalongs reveals names like 200₡Sox and Summer of Lace. Other knitalongs are timed to coincide with important events, such as a political knit-in coinciding with a G8 Summit.

Some, like Stitch N' Pitch (see page 30) or Spin Out, a fiber spinning meet-up that took place in New York City, are intended to last only a single day. A knitting cruise to Alaska or a knitting camp-out might last a week. An online KAL focused on a complex sweater pattern might last several months, giving all the participants time to share the process. Often in-person knitting groups do not have an announced deadline, and operate more like book clubs, lasting for years as the membership evolves.

WHAT ARE THE GUIDELINES?

People want "the rules." If you are holding a knitalong that's any more structured than a weekly meet-up, people will want to know such things as exactly how to sign up, what patterns they're supposed to use and where to get them, when the KAL officially starts and ends, how to report their progress, and more. Thinking about these things ahead of time—before you announce your KAL idea to the public—will make the process smoother for everyone.

HOW WILL YOU USE TECHNOLOGY TO MAKE KNITTING TOGETHER MORE FUN AND EASY?

Even if it's a tin can and string leading to your neighbor's window, you will probably use some kind of technology to plan and coordinate your KAL. Ask yourself what level of technology is right for you and your group. Phones only? Or a multi-user, interactive online space?

If it's the latter, you can learn from online KALs gone by. An overall principle you may want to strive for is to eliminate administrative work. Use any kind of free service that keeps you from having to juggle names on a spreadsheet or from hosting photographs on your own computer and website. You can find such services by using an Internet search engine. Perhaps the easiest and best way of all is to e-mail someone who is hosting a KAL that looks like it's about your style and speed, and ask how they are handling it technically.

If you're not familiar or comfortable with the technology that's available, ask the people in your knitalong or knitting group if there's someone who is. Or perhaps even find a friend outside the knitting circle who is willing to pitch in.

HOW WILL YOU SHARE YOUR WORK?

As a knitalong organizer, part of your job is to make it easy and fun for people to share what they're making. If you meet in person, it's obviously easy. Online knitalong managers face more of a challenge, but also enjoy a wide

KAL Words of Wisdom

❋ "Try to keep it personal," says Stephanie Pearl-McPhee, knitter and author from Toronto, who created the Knitting Olympics. "Make the successes flexible so that knitters at all levels can knit along according to their own abilities. There's nothing like setting it up so that almost everybody is a winner."

❋ "Be flexible," says Kay Gardiner, coauthor of *Mason-Dixon Knitting*, who collected more than 1,000 knitted squares in her Manhattan apartment to create charity blankets for Afghans for Afghans. "Other people will take your idea and add their own ideas that make it much better."

❋ "A good KAL, to my mind, is one that unifies, yet allows people to deviate in a way that shows their personal creativity and vision," says Julia Trice from Winter, California—knitter, designer, and cofounder of Create Along, an online knitalong for people who are dreaming up original knitting designs.

❋ Ask for technical help. "Luckily we had two amazingly talented computer whizzes on our team," says Scout, founder of the Dye-O-Rama swap. She recommends sites like Swapbot.com to eliminate some of the tedium. "It's a really great program that lets people sign up for a swap and then randomly picks partners for you."

❋ Photos can make a huge difference to the tenor and amount of feedback a knitter gets when participating in an online KAL. Caro Sheridan of the blog Split Yarn advises using natural light, your camera's macro setting, a "teeny" inexpensive tripod, and a 42-cent sheet of white poster board to create a backdrop. The final step, she says, is using a program like Photoshop to tweak the results. "I suggest giving the auto-levels and auto-color correction features a try. It's amazing the difference they can make."

❋ Recognize knitters and give them some fame. Ann Shayne and Kay Gardiner of *Mason-Dixon Knitting*, took the time to document charity afghan squares as they came rolling in. They posted pictures and notes in the margin of their blog almost daily, so people saw their contributions arriving and felt acknowledged. "It made a huge difference," says Kay.

❋ "The only knitalongs I found myself sticking with were those with some sort of reward at the end," confesses Sock-A-Month cohost and knitting designer Chrissy Gardiner. She believes prizes of sock yarn are crucial to her KAL's success. "I usually put out a couple calls for yarn donations during each SAM and participants are very generous with their stashes, which helps to cover the expense of all those prizes."

range of choices, including free mapping software that plots your knitalong on a world map, photo-sharing web-sites that allow you to create photo mosaics, multiple-user blogs that allow many knitters to post journal entries, and e-mail discussion groups where ideas can fly as fast as you can say "Got mail."

WILL YOU OFFER ANY OTHER PERKS?

Many knitalongs include random prize drawings to encour-age people to show up on a special night at the LYS, finish a scarf or hat or pair of socks by the deadline, or get an afghan square into the organizer's hands by a certain date. Often, prizes will include donations of yarn, needles, knit-ting tools, books, magazines, and more, from the organizer herself or from other knitalongers.

In the case of our State Fair Knitalong (see page 96), the yarn store Abundant Yarn & Dyeworks worked together with us to host the knitalong and provided door prizes—in-cluding kits to make felted bags—for people who came to the kickoff event. For the duration of the knitalong, their café offered a discount to anyone who was signed up for the KAL.

Beyond yarn and in-hand prizes, there are online perks that are free and easy for the organizer and that provide a sense of belonging and accomplishment for knitters. Stephanie Pearl-McPhee offered a simple digital picture of a gold medal as the carrot for her Knitting Olym-pics athletes (see page 102). The organizers of the 52 Pair Plunge, an online sock knitalong that challenges partici-pants to knit fifty-two pairs of socks in one year, provide 52 Pair Plunge progress bars—little graphic documents that participants can download and use to brag about how far they are on their sock journey. These little touches make knitalongers feel included, noticed, and cared for, and they keep the KAL feeling new and dynamic over time.

Launching a KAL: At a Glance

Here's a quick checklist to help you get a knitalong started.

Choose a focus, such as pattern, yarn, color, project, challenge, or simple companionship.

Choose a venue—online or in person or a combination of both.

Choose a place and time.

Promote your KAL.

Add some door prizes and recognition.

Use technology to make your life easier, and make your KAL more fun for everyone.

Make show-and-tell an important part of the experience.

Enjoy!

Abbreviations

BO: Bind off

Ch: Chain

Circ: Circular

CO: Cast on

Dcd (double centered decrease): Slip next 2 sts together knitwise to right-hand needle, k1, pass 2 slipped sts over knit stitch.

Dpn(s): Double-pointed needle(s)

K: Knit

K1-f/b: Knit into front loop and back loop of same stitch to increase one stitch.

K1-tbl: Knit one stitch through the back loop, twisting the stitch.

K2tog: Knit 2 sts together.

K3tog: Knit 3 sts together.

M1 or M1-l (make 1-left slanting): With the tip of the left-hand needle inserted from front to back, lift the strand between the two needles onto the left-hand needle; knit the strand through the back loop to increase one stitch.

M1-p (make 1 purlwise): With the tip of the left-hand needle inserted from back to front, lift the strand between the two needles onto the left-hand needle; purl the strand through the front loop to increase one stitch.

P: Purl

P1-f/b: Purl into front loop and back loop of same stitch to increase one stitch.

P2tog: Purl 2 sts together.

Pm: Place marker

Psso (pass slipped stitch over): Pass slipped st on right-hand needle over the sts indicated in the instructions, as in binding off.

Rem: Remain(ing)

Rep: Repeat

Rnd: Round

RS: Right side

Sc(s): Single crochet(s)

Skp (slip, knit, pass): Slip next st knitwise to right-hand needle, k1, pass slipped st over knit st.

Sl (slip): Slip stitch(es) as if to purl, unless otherwise specified.

Sl st (crochet slip stitch): Insert hook in st, yarn over hook, and draw through loop on hook.

Sm: Slip marker

Ssk (slip, slip, knit): Slip the next 2 sts to the right-hand needle one at a time as if to knit; return them back to left-hand needle one at a time in their new orientation; knit them together through the back loops.

St(s): Stitch(es)

Tbl: Through the back loop

Tog: Together

WS: Wrong side

Yo: Yarn over (see Special Techniques)

Special Techniques

Backward Loop CO: Make a slip knot with the working yarn and place it on the right-hand needle [first st CO], * wind yarn around thumb clockwise, insert right-hand needle into the front of the loop on thumb, remove thumb and tighten st on needle; repeat from * for remaining sts to be CO, or for casting on at the end of a row in progress.

Garter Stitch: Knit every row when working straight; knit 1 round, purl 1 round when working circular.

I-Cord: Using a double-pointed needle, cast on or pick up the required number of sts; the working yarn will be at the left end of the needle. * Transfer the needle with the sts to your left hand, bring the yarn around behind the work to the right end; using a second double-pointed needle, knit the sts from right to left, pulling the yarn from left to right for the first st; do not turn. Slide the sts to the opposite end of the needle; repeat from * until the I-Cord is the length desired. Note: After a few rows, the tubular shape will become apparent.

Applied I-Cord: Using a double-pointed needle, cast on or pick up the required number of sts; the working yarn will be at the left end of the needle. Transfer the needle with the sts to your left hand, bring the yarn around behind the work to the right end; using a second double-pointed needle, knit the sts from right to left, pulling the yarn from left to right for the first st. Turn piece so that WS is facing, pick and knit 1 st from edge to which I-Cord will be applied. * Slide the sts to the opposite end of the needle, knit to the last 2 sts, k2, k2tog, pick up and knit 1 st from edge; repeat from * around the entire edge to which the I-Cord is to be applied, working even rows between pick-up rows if necessary so that I-Cord is smooth. When working around a corner, work 2 or 3 successive pick-up rows into the corner stitch to allow the I-Cord to turn the corner smoothly.

Intarsia Colorwork Method: Use a separate length of yarn for each color section; you may wind yarn onto bobbins to make color changes easier. When changing colors, bring the new yarn up and to the right of the yarn just used to twist the yarns and prevent leaving a hole; do not carry colors not in use across the back of the work.

Kitchener Stitch: Using a blunt yarn needle, thread a length of yarn approximately 4 times the length of the section to be joined. Hold the pieces to be joined wrong sides together, with the needles holding the sts parallel, both ends pointing in the same direction. Working from right to left, insert yarn needle into first st on front needle as if to purl, pull yarn through, leaving st on needle; insert yarn needle into first st on back needle as if to knit, pull yarn through, leaving st on needle; *insert yarn needle into first st on front needle as if to knit, pull yarn through, remove st from needle; insert yarn needle into next st on front needle as if to purl, pull yarn through, leave st on needle; insert yarn needle into first st on back needle as if to purl, pull yarn through, remove st from needle; insert yarn needle into next st on back needle as if to knit, pull yarn through, leave st on needle. Repeat from *, working 3 or 4 sts at a time, then go back and adjust tension to match the pieces being joined. When 1 st remains on each needle, cut yarn and pass through last 2 sts to fasten off.

Long-Tail (Thumb) CO: Leaving tail with about 1" of yarn for each st to be cast-on, make a slip knot in the yarn and place it on the right-hand needle, with the tail end to the front and the working end to the back. Insert the thumb and forefinger of your left hand between the strands of yarn so that the working end is around your forefinger, and the tail end is around your thumb "slingshot" fashion; * insert the tip of the right-hand needle into the front loop on the thumb, hook the strand of yarn coming from the forefinger from back to front, and draw it through the loop on your thumb; remove your thumb from the loop and pull on the working yarn to tighten the new st on the right-hand needle; return your thumb and forefinger to their original positions, and repeat from * for remaining sts to be CO.

Overhand Braid: Separate ends into 3 even groups.
Step 1: Working right to left, take right group over center group.
Step 2: Working left to right, take left group over new center group.
Repeat Steps 1 and 2 to 2" from end of strands or to desired length. Tie overhand knot to secure and cut ends.

Reading Charts: Unless otherwise specified in the instructions, when working straight, charts are read from right to left for RS rows, from left to right for WS rows. Row numbers are written at the beginning of each row. Numbers on the right indicate RS rows; numbers on the left indicate WS rows. When working circular, all rounds are read from right to left.

Reverse Stockinette Stitch (Rev St st): Purl on RS rows, knit on WS rows when working straight; purl every round when working circular.

Ribbing: Although rib stitch patterns use different numbers of sts, all are worked in the same way, whether straight or circular. The instructions will specify how many sts to knit or purl; the example below uses k1, p1.
Row/Rnd 1: * K1, p1; repeat from * across (end k1 if an odd number of sts).
Row/Rnd 2: Knit the knit sts and purl the purl sts as they face you.
Repeat Row/Rnd 2 for rib st.

Seed Stitch
Row/Rnd 1: * K1, p1; repeat from * across (end k1 if an odd number of sts).
Row/Rnd 2: Knit the purls and purl the knits as they face you. Repeat Row/Rnd 2 for Seed st.

Stockinette Stitch (St st): Knit on RS rows, purl on WS rows when working straight; knit every round when working circular.

Stranded (Fair Isle) Colorwork Method: When more than one color is used per row, carry color(s) not in use loosely across the WS of work. Be sure to secure all colors at beginning and end of rows to prevent holes.

Three-Needle BO: Place the sts to be joined onto two same-size needles; hold the pieces to be joined with the right sides facing each other and the needles parallel, both pointing to the right. Holding both needles in your left hand, using working yarn and a third needle same size or one size larger, insert third needle into first st on front needle, then into first st on back needle; knit these two sts together; * knit next st from each needle together (two sts on right-hand needle); pass first st over second st to BO one st. Repeat from * until one st remains on third needle; cut yarn and fasten off.

Yarn Over (Yo): Bring yarn forward (to the purl position), then place it in position to work the next st. If next st is to be knit, bring yarn over the needle and knit; if next st is to be purled, bring yarn over the needle and then forward again to the purl position and purl. Work the yarn over in pattern on the next row unless instructed otherwise.

Sources for Supplies

ABUNDANT YARN
& DYEWORKS
8524 SE 17th Ave.
Portland, OR 97202
503-258-9276
www.abundantyarn.com

ARAUCANIA
Dist. by Knitting Fever
PO Box 336
315 Bayview Ave.
Amityville, NY 11701
516-546-3600
www.knittingfever.com

BERROCO
14 Elmdale Rd.
PO Box 367
Uxbridge, MA 01569
508-278-2527
www.berroco.com

BLUE MOON FIBER
ARTS, INC.
866-802-9687
www.bluemoonfiberarts.com

BLUE SKY ALPACAS, INC
PO Box 88
Cedar, MN 55011
888-460-8862
www.blueskyalpacas.com

BROWN SHEEP
COMPANY, INC.
100662 County Rd. 16
Mitchell, NE 69357
800-826-9136
www.brownsheep.com

CASCADE YARNS
1224 Andover Park East
Tukwila, WA 98188
800-548-1048
www.cascadeyarns.com

CLASSIC ELITE YARNS,
INC.
122 Western Ave.
Lowell, MA 01851
978-453-2837
www.classiceliteyarns.com

DALE OF NORWAY, INC.
4750 Shelburne Rd.,
Suite 20
Shelburne, VT 05482
802-383-0132
www.daleyarns.com

DEBBIE BLISS
Dist. by Knitting Fever
PO Box 336
315 Bayview Ave.
Amityville, NY 11701
516-546-3600
www.knittingfever.com

FROG TREE YARNS
PO Box 1119
East Dennis, MA 02641
508-385-8862
www.frogtreeyarns.com

KOIGU
Koigu Wool Designs
PO Box 158
Chatsworth, ON N0H1G0
Canada
888-765-WOOL
www.koigu.com

LFN TEXTILES
1700 West Irving Park Road,
Suite 205B
Chicago, IL 60613
812-682-3733
www.lfntextiles.com

LOUET
3425 Hands Rd.
Prescott, ON K0E1T0
Canada
613-925-4502
www.louet.com

MALABRIGO
786-866-6187
www.malabrigoyarn.com

MANOS DEL URUGUAY
Dist. by Fairmount Fibers
915 N. 28th St.
Philadelphia, PA 19130
888-566-9970
www.fairmountfibers.com

NORO
Dist. by Knitting Fever
PO Box 336
315 Bayview Ave.
Amityville, NY 11701
516-546-3600
www.knittingfever.com

ROWAN CLASSIC YARNS
(RYC)
Dist. by Westminster Fibers
165 Ledge St.
Nashua, NH 03060
800-445-9276
www.westminsterfibers.com
www.ryclassic.com

SHIBUI KNITS
503-595-5898
www.shibuiknits.com

TAHKI STACY CHARLES,
INC.
70-30 80th St. Building 36
Ridgewood, NY 11385
800-338-YARN
www.tahkistacycharles.com